THE CHER SCRAPBOOK

THE
CHER SCRAPBOOK

Mary Anne Cassata

CITADEL PRESS
Kensington Publishing Corp.
www.kensingtonbooks.com

CITADEL PRESS BOOKS are published by

Kensington Publishing Corp.
850 Third Avenue
New York, NY 10022

All Kensington titles, imprints, and distributed lines are available at special quantity discounts for bulk purchases for sales promotions, premiums, fund-raising, educational, or institutional use. Special book excerpts or customized printings can also be created to fit specific needs. For details, write or phone the office of the Kensington special sales manager: Kensington Publishing Corp., 850 Third Avenue, New York, NY 10022, attn: Special Sales Department, phone 1-800-221-2647.

CITADEL PRESS is Reg. U.S. Pat. & TM Off.
The Citadel Logo is a trademark of Kensington Publishing Corp.

Designed by Anne Ricigliano/Planet Patti, Inc.

First printing: November 2002

10 9 8 7 6 5 4 3 2

Printed in the United States of America

Library of Congress Control Number: 2002104314

ISBN 0-8065-2343-3

Dedicated to the memory of Sonny Bono,
who through his songs and as part of Sonny & Cher
has provided the world with wonderful memories

CONTENTS

Sonny & Cher

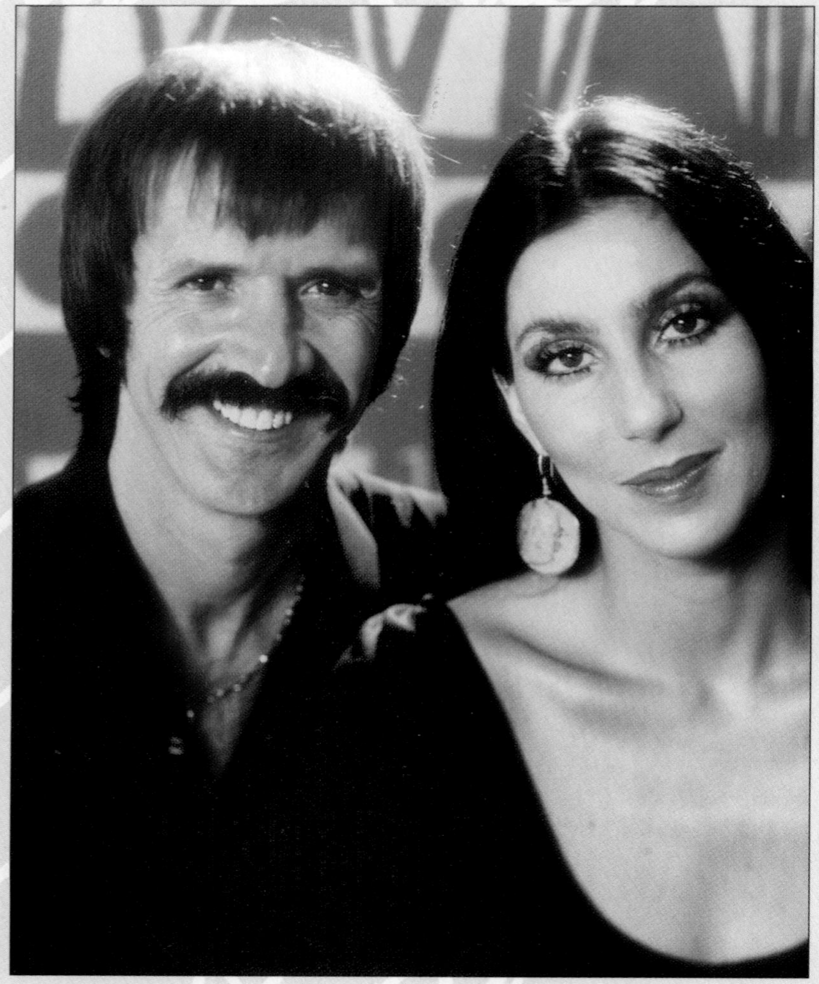

PREFACE

Baby Don't Go

I still love Sonny & Cher. Do you know what I mean? I always liked them as an act. I was always able to separate myself from Sonny & Cher. I will always have a fondness for that time and part of my life. When Cher and I get together, there's some kind of mystical magic that occurs. It must come from God. . . . I give Cher a lot of credit. I am very proud of her. What she has she has certainly worked hard for and certainly deserves.

—Sonny Bono to Mary Anne Cassata, 1987

was nine years old the first time I saw and heard Sonny & Cher sing "Baby Don't Go" playing on my pretty, pink, transistor radio. I was immediately drawn to the words written by Sonny Bono and identified with the young girl's sad plight of poverty and having a mother and a father that she hardly knew at all. Having no money and buying your clothes at a second-hand store is never any fun either, and who wants to stay in a town where you are laughed at for being poor and the product of a broken home?

Flash forward twelve years—as I make my way from the old upstate town I'm from to the big city of Manhattan, I think of how this new beginning will help leave my tears behind and how no one here will know how much I have cried—just like the words from the song. I loved Sonny & Cher then as much as I do today. "Baby Don't Go" is still my favorite song. I remember seeing them in the sixties on *American Bandstand* and *Hullabaloo*— Sonny with his Caesar haircut and fur vest and Cher in her flashy bell-bottom pants. What an unforgettable fashion statement they made at the time!

In the seventies, like the rest of America, I couldn't wait for the *Sonny & Cher Comedy Hour* to be on. I wondered every week what outrageous Bob Mackie gown Cher was going to wear this time. Hope it's the Indian Squaw, Electric Feathers or maybe the LaPlume one. Will Cher be singing one of those smoky torch ballads like "The Man That Got Away" or "Just For a Thrill" or will it be one of her classic hits like "Gypsies, Tramps and Thieves," "Dark Lady" or "Half Breed"? Whatever she sang or wore on the show would be talked about till the following week.

In 1975 I wrote for a local entertainment publication. One of the first records I reviewed was *Stars*, which featured the single "Geronimo's Cadillac." Two years later, I was on assignment to review Sonny & Cher at a new theater-in-the-round called Melody Fair. At the time, of course, they were already divorced and traveled in separate cars to the venue. That was a weird sight to witness. As members of the local press, a few of us were invited backstage for what is called a "meet and greet." It was the first time I had met them and I will never forget how friendly they were to the press and of course how perfectly glamorous Cher looked in a gold-sequined Mackie outfit. It was thrilling to be so close to Cher and at the same time working in a professional capacity. I was still new to my craft and still learning the ropes, and of course I wanted to appear as professional as possible.

By 1980 I was working in Manhattan as a freelance entertainment writer and wrangled an assignment to interview Cher, who was now with the rock band Black Rose. Time was limited and I could only ask a few questions—but, hey, that was enough for me. Cher, as I had hoped, was friendly and seemed genuinely happy to talk about her new venture as a hard-rock artist. I remember telling her I liked the way her voice sounded on the song titled "Julie," which was written by Bernie Taupin.

From 1983 to 1988 I went from a freelance writer to a magazine editor when I was hired by D.S. Magazines—a teen-star publication company that was originally owned by Laufer Publications. Working with magazine titles like *Tiger Beat* and *Star!*, I had full access to the old Laufer files from the sixties and seventies. What a treat, too! The Sonny & Cher section of the files, which could rival my own personal collection included pages of unused Sonny & Cher interview transcripts, rare press information and never-before-seen photos from *Rona Barrett's Hollywood* and *Tattle Tales* magazines. Remember all those Sonny & Cher pictures blazing across the covers? I found many of these in the files with the original crop marks made by the magazine designers as well as various notes from Rona Barrett's own handwriting on the original, typed manuscripts.

Besides the teen publications, D.S. Magazines also had an entertainment book division, for which I was required to write biography books on whatever star was hot at the time. In the mid-eighties it was Michael J. Fox and the big reunion of the Monkees. In early 1988, when I was asked

to write about Cher, it was one of the happiest days of my life. I had waited so long to write a biography book on Cher. Sonny, not yet Mayor Bono of Palm Springs at the time, even granted me an interview—the first of three that would follow over the next few years.

I had only two weeks to churn out a manuscript because Cher was expected to win an Oscar for *Moonstruck*. It was my job to have the manuscript ready up to that point—which I did—thanks in part to Sonny's valuable contributions and, of course, old, reliable files that even included a forty-page document of Sonny & Cher's divorce papers. However, disappointment was soon to set in. My softcover trade book simply titled *Cher!* (the cover featured Cher from the "Vamp" segment), which included rare photos and behind-the-scenes information, was published a couple of months later and quickly disappeared off the shelves. I couldn't believe it, nor understand why. The reason or reasons were never fully explained to me by the publisher. Looking back, I can only assume either the timing wasn't right or that maybe Cher had planned to publish her own book at some point in the near future. Today, every so often a friend will e-mail me and say they've seen a rare copy on eBay selling for $75 (the original cover price was $5.95). In any case, I have been writing this new book for over sixteen years. I tried to sell an updated version of the original book, but no publisher seemed interested since by that time there were already so many Cher biographies on the market. So, in the last few years, I decided to change the book's direction and make it a tribute to Cher's life and career. After all, what was I supposed to do with my thirty-year-plus collection that has moved with me seven times since 1980? I might as well put it to good use, right? I had also covered Cher's various career moves over the years and now my enormous collection had expanded to personally owning clothes and jewelry once worn and owned by Cher.

So, the purpose of this book is to celebrate the life and career of a woman who inspires millions of people, and instills a sense of hope through her songs, live performances, film appearances, her personal outlook on life, and more. Cher—this single word word says it all.

Today, Cher is undeniably still the hardest-working woman in show business. How many entertainers have successfully re-invented themselves for new generations of fans? From her days with Sonny Bono in the sixties to becoming a "diva" in the nineties, Cher is a true survivor. Four decades of records, concerts, television, films, Broadway, and books, this pop-culture phenomenon at age fifty-six shows absolutely no sign of slowing down. How much more is there to learn about Cher that we don't know already? You'd be surprised. Though the public has witnessed every shock and every resurgence in her incredible life and lengthy career, there are still new things to learn about this amazing woman, christened Cherilyn Sarkisian.

So, what's to love about Cher? Her songs, her Bob Mackie costumes, her concert performances, her acting, and her men! Why does Cher have millions of fans who truly care about her? As longtime fans already know, Cher's astounding talent is bigger than life itself. Her honesty and humanity are qualities that make this astonishing woman so easily likable. Perhaps her incomparability lies in such an enchanting blend of peak talent and flair.

The *Cher Scrapbook* is full of unforgettable memories, achievements, projects, people, and special moments in time. It is my fondest wish that all the Cher fans out there that read this book will be as inspired as I always have been by this gracious, beautiful and kind woman.

—Mary Anne Cassata
May 8, 2002

THE CHER SCRAPBOOK

Cher dropped out of high school to study acting.

CHAPTER ONE

The Cher Basics

Full Real Name: Cherilyn Sarkisian LaPierre (she was adopted by her mother's third husband, Gilbert LaPierre, and took his last name).

Official Legal Name: Cher (in the late seventies she legally changed her name to simply "Cher" because she only wanted to be known by a one-word name).

Nicknames: Her family calls her C., Ma, and Cherilyn.

Occupation: Singer, actress, producer, director, diva.

Date of Birth: May 20, 1946.

Birthplace: El Centro, California.

Parents' Names: Georgia Holt and John Sarkisian (father is deceased); stepfathers—John Southhall was married to Cher's mother in the early 1950s and Gilbert LaPierre became Georgia's fifth husband in 1961.

Siblings: One half-sister, Georgianne LaPierre.

Education: Dropped out of high school; studied acting with Jeff Corey.

Current Boyfriend: She is rumored to be secretly reunited with Rob Camilletti for over a year now, but none of her people will confirm it. But it is confirmed that he lives in her Malibu mansion and goes to work as a bartender each night.

(Select) Former Boyfriends: Les Dudek, Gene Simmons, Richie Sambora, Val Kilmer, Josh Donen, Tom Cruise, Rob Camilletti, and David Geffen.

Height: Five feet, seven and one half inches.

Weight: She is said to weigh about 125 now that she's more athletic, but in her most stressful times on the *Sonny & Cher* set, she weighed only 98 pounds! She averaged 103 pounds by the time she did the *Cher* show.

Hair Color: Originally black, but now varies from pink to blond to black again (plus, she usually sports wigs for most public appearances).

Worst Hair Disaster: Supposedly lost most of her hair after a bad dye job in the early seventies, but it grew back.

Eyes: Brown.

Clothes Size: Six.

Religion: Considers herself to be very spiritual, but not to be of a specific religion.

Astrological Sign: Taurus.

Marital Status: Official press information from the early sixties to the the mid-seventies stated that Sonny & Cher married October 27, 1964, in Tijuana, Mexico. These reports later proved to be fabricated. In reality, Cher herself "married" them in the bathroom of their first home, where they simply exchanged rings and vows without the presence of family, friends, witnesses, or a minister. Cher divorced Sonny in 1975. She married musician Greg Allman on June 30, 1975, in Las Vegas, Nevada; they divorced later that same year.

Children: Two: Chastity Sun Bono and Elijah Blue Allman.

Best Friend: Paulette Betts (for the past thirty years).

Political Affiliation: Democrat (although Cher has also admitted to not having any political affiliation).

Pets: Over the years, several cats and dogs.

Personal Motto: "I don't answer to anyone but God and myself."

Favorite Pastimes: Shopping, reading, redecorating, real estate investing. It is said she has remodeled more than a dozen Malibu and Beverly Hills estates, made a killing on each sale).

Favorite Charity: Children's Craniofacial Association.

First Job: Working in See's Candy store on Sunset Boulevard when she was sixteen.

Self-Admitted Worst Career Moves: Doing an infomercial for a friend's haircare products; acting in the film *Faithful*; performing with Black Rose.

First Song Ever Recorded: "Ringo, I Love You" under the name of Bonnie Jo Mason on Annette Records in 1965. (Before that, she recorded background vocals on many Phil Spector produced recordings including the super hit "Da Doo Ron Ron" by the Crystals).

First Single Released as Caesar & Cleo: "The Letter" on Vault Records in 1965.

First Single Released as Sonny & Cher: "Just You" on Atco Records in 1965.

First Single Released as Cherilyn: "Dream Baby" on Imperial Records in 1965.

Exotic, luscious, and beautiful is how a seventies film director once described Cher.

First Single Released as Cher: "All I Really Want to Do" on Imperial Records in 1965.

Film Credits: *Wild on the Beach* (1965); *Good Times* (1967); *Chastity* (1969); *Come Back to the 5 & Dime, Jimmy Dean, Jimmy Dean* (1982); *Silkwood* (1983); *Mask* (1985); *Moonstruck* (1987); *Suspect* (1987); *Witches of Eastwick* (1987), *Mermaids* (1990); *The Player* (1992); *Ready to Wear* (1994); *Faithful* (1996); *If These Walls Could Talk* (1996, Showtime original movie, which she also directed), and *Tea With Mussolini* (1999).

(Select) Television Appearances: *Cher* (1975); *Cher Special* (1978); *Cher and Other Fantasies* (1979); *Cher—A Celebration at Caesar's Palace* (1983); *Cher Extravaganza at the Mirage* (1991); *Comic Relief: Behind the Nose* (1995); *Happy Birthday Elizabeth: a Celebration of Life* (1997); *Sonny & Me . . . Cher Remembers* (1998); 26th Annual American Music Awards (1998); *Cher Live in Las Vegas* (1999); *VH-1 Divas Live* (1999); *AFI's 100 Years, 100 Stars* (1999); *Cher Live in Concert* (1999); and *I Love Lucy's 50th Anniversary Special* (2001).

(Select) Awards: Grammy for Best Pop Dance Recording—"Believe" (1999); Best Actress Academy Award for her role in *Moonstruck* opposite Nicholas Cage (1988); Cannes Film Festival Award for Best Actress in *Mask* (1985); four Golden Globes (for *Moonstruck*, *Mask*, *Silkwood*, and *Witches of Eastwick*); A Golden Globe for Best TV Actress in Musical or Comedy for *The Sonny & Cher Comedy Hour* (1973).

Most Fun Award: Harvard Hasty Pudding Award for "Woman of the Year" (1985).

TV Series: *The Sonny & Cher Comedy Hour*

At the premiere of *Silkwood*.

Over three thousand fans showed up at a New York City Sam Goody to support Cher when her *It's a Man's World* was released in 1995.

(1971–1974); *Cher* (1975–1976); *The Sonny & Cher Show* (1976–1977).

Most Successful Album: *Believe* (2000).

Most Successful Single: "Believe," which reached platinum status.

Least Successful Album: 1975's *Stars* (the album was panned by *Rolling Stone* magazine, not even getting one star). However, *Stars* ranks high among longtime fans as one of her best albums of the seventies.

Least Successful Single: That's a toss up. Either "I Love You Ringo" (under the name Bonnie Jo Mason) from 1965 or "Rudy" from 1982.

Stage Clothes: Designed by herself in the early days and sewn up by a Hollywood tailor. Have been designed by Bob Mackie since 1970. (A lot of Cher's more popular television and stage clothes like the Indian and Laverne outfits were on display at New York's Parson School of Design in 1999.)

The Reinvention of Cher

Move over, Madonna. While the younger MTV set have always called her the "Queen of Reinvention," Cher fans know who the real queen is. From the time she was a teen, hanging on the arm of aspiring songwriter/record producer Sonny Bono, to recent times, when she enjoyed a Top ten Billboard chart position with her last single, "Song for the Lonely," Cher has changed her image many times. But is it ever enough? Cynical media critics have often said that at age fifty-six Cher should "give it up" and just "let herself get old like everyone else." But she refuses to let that happen. Cher certainly has the means never to work again and to enjoy the rest of her life in the style she is accustomed to, but she always wants more, and always wants to appeal to the younger

Cher's had many lives. Not all of them successful, but all interesting. In the end, the Dark Lady is still as triumphant as ever.

entertainment market. You'll never find her doing something smarmy like singing Bee Gees covers in a Las Vegas lounge or doing dinner theater in suburban Ohio.

Cher's first big reinvention came at age sixteen. She was basically a normal teen (her only real sign of rebellion at the time, according to her mother, Georgia Holt, was that she dated much older men). Cher met newly separated Sonny Bono in late 1962 after she had a brief fling with actor Warren Beatty. Cher now concedes in inter-

Cher refers to her latest reinvention as "probably my fifth phase. I've had so many rebirths, I should come with my own midwife by now."

views that she and Sonny were "both odd characters at the time," but once the dynamic duo had a serious recording deal with Atlantic, they put their freak flags at high mast with furry vests, bell bottoms, wide belts, and bangs that obstructed their eyesight. Even back then, Cher acknowledged that she had a Cleopatralike look, and emphasized it with mile-long eyeliner and pale foundation and lips. She became a poster child for girls that were different (those who didn't have that all-American, blond-haired, blue-eyed look that was so popular in Hollywood at the time).

The sixties moved on, and Sonny & Cher became has-beens in 1968. They had a good three-year run of hits but times were changing, and their antidrug stance and lovey-dovey pop hits just seemed obsolete once Viet Nam was in full force and heavier acts like Jimi Hendrix and the Doors became popular. At this time, Cher changed her image by appearing in Sonny's self-produced movie vehicle, which was designed for her talents. It was titled *Chastity*, and Cher played a wild runaway. But the hip flick was anything but a runaway hit.

Cher spent 1969 through 1971 recording an assortment of solo albums that didn't really go anywhere, and Sonny & Cher did the Vegas circuit until they were offered a summer replacement series in 1971 by CBS. Cher was dismayed to find out that Sonny still wanted to do the Vegas shows on weekends, even though the *Sonny & Cher Comedy Hour* was a huge success.

Cher's second reinvention arrived in the

form of ultimate glamour woman—the bare-midriffed "mannequin" fueled by the glitzy fashion designs of Bob Mackie. In *TV Guide*, she was described as being "rich hippie chic," and Mackie was the first designer to bring "barely there" gowns to television audiences. Mackie has stated that Cher was in such perfect shape that nothing ever looked vulgar on her, even if it was an outfit that looked like three Band-Aids with a few sequins sewn on.

"Cher is an invention. I invented someone who is funny and interesting. I think you can invent your life as you go along."

This is Cher's most popular era in the minds of older Americans, most likely because the gowns were so memorable and still appear in various fashion retrospectives around the country today.

When Cher and Sonny divorced in 1975, and they no longer worked on TV together, Cher reinvented herself again. Serious fans were not thrilled when the *Comedy Hour* transformed into the *Sonny & Cher Show*, featuring a divorced couple and Cher now carrying her new husband's Gregg Allman, child.

The Dark Lady was feeling independent for the first time in her life, and her new attitude radiated physically. On occasion, she wore casual outfits on the show, which were usually tight jeans paired with a more subdued Mackie spangled blouse. From 1977 to 1979, when the disco era was in full bloom, Cher was reinvented as disco diva supreme. She was often seen at Los Angeles roller discos and crooning Casablanca hits like "Take Me Home," "Wasn't It Good?," and "Hell on Wheels." She was seen in New York at the famed Studio 54, but it turned out that she

The one constant thing about Cher is change.

was not the disco queen everyone took her for. By this time, Cher was divorced from Gregg Allman and dating Kiss bassist Gene Simmons. Deep down inside, Cher has always possessed a wild, gypsy, rock and roll heart.

Cher's music career was put on hold as her acting career took off in the early 1980s. Her next reinvention was as a serious actress, thanks to the help of one of her mother's dear old friends "in the business," director Robert Altman. Cher temporarily moved to New York and took a leading role in the critically acclaimed Broadway play *Come Back to the 5 & Dime, Jimmy Dean, Jimmy Dean,* and eventually re-created the role on-screen (directed by Altman). For the role, the thirty-five-year-old, serious, actress-minded Cher portrayed a Southern waitress opposite veteran actresses Sandy Dennis and Karen Black.

More films followed: *Mask, Silkwood, Suspect,* and *Moonstruck.*

When she won an Oscar for *Moonstruck,* she was wearing a glitzy, black-sequined Mackie gown, proving that although she took on "salt of the earth" type roles in the movies, deep down she was a true fashionista who wanted to show off a little. Arguably, the closest Cher ever got to being glamorous on-screen was as a jet-setting American socialite transplanted in Italy during World War II in *Tea With Mussolini.* The chinchilla-trimmed cashmere suit she donned for the role is fodder for the movie wardrobe hall of fame, even though no one but the most hardcore members of the fashion press noticed it.

While enjoying a string of great movie roles in the mid eighties, Cher created an alter ego for herself as fitness guru, donning some of the fanciest workout outfits the world has ever seen—including one with a metal mesh top that she appeared in for a Bally's advertisement. Cher's glamorous gown-donning self still surfaced though, most noticeably when promoting her signature fragrance Uninhibited, which is now a big fan collectible.

Cher had reinvented herself yet again by the time the nineties rolled in. She became part pop diva, part goth goddess, and part Mrs. Robinson (that is, the sexy older woman). When she appeared in Mackie's barest design ever in the sailor-enhanced "If I Could Turn Back Time" video, she stumbled into newfound pop fame after being in a missing-hit funk for nearly a decade. That outfit is still talked about to this day, and the scene of the sailors cheering on Cher's bare, tattooed backside will forever be imbedded in the minds of pop-music fans.

From the early nineties through the new millennium, Cher has maintained mostly a goth image when it comes to fashion, with a little bit of glam-biker thrown in for good measure. However, at her concerts, there are at least eight to ten costume changes that depict Cher's every fashion mode. She is said to have picked up the biker edge while married to Greg Allman, who got her into Harleys. Even today, at least once a year, Cher rides in motorcycle events on her bike to raise money for the Craniofacial Association.

No one better than Cher has ability to reinvent herself and change her style to match the times. Without a doubt this is surely the reason why Cher's musical career has spanned four decades and shows no signs of slowing down.

Where the goth comes in is questionable, although while dating Gene Simmons, she probably encountered heavy metal friends of his such as Ozzy Osbourne, who helped bring the genre to the U.S. Cher's love of goth is most openly displayed in her Sanctuary catalog, which originated in the late nineties but is now out of print. For that catalog, Cher shopped around the world for exotic items that could be brought back stateside for sales to the masses. Some items were "genuine" pieces purchased in bulk for catalog sales, and some were reproductions of expensive items she bought for her personal use.

Cher also holds a special place in the hair-color hall of fame, outdoing Madonna in terms of how often she changes the hue of her tresses. Lately, she sports wigs and can probably rival Dolly Parton in that arena. Cher has a climate-controlled room in her Malibu home where she keeps her expensive "rugs" and famous Mackie gowns. As one cartoon said, "After the nuclear bomb is dropped, what will be left are cockroaches and Cher." As long as she keeps reinventing herself in new, exciting ways, fans will always be mesmerized.

But honestly, even if she became "Just Plain Cher" and ceased to be a fashion horse and tress trendsetter, fans would still love her. Cher has shown her "plain" side most recently in her "Song for the Lonely" video where she walks around Manhattan wearing a wool hat and parka with just a bunch of "regular folk"; fans don't seem to mind that she's not wearing a glamorous frock or baring her physical assets.

It's important to keep in mind that Cher is about much more than just looks and talent.

When she reinvents herself, very often it has to do with her desire to grow spiritually or support a cause she feels strongly about. When she directed *If These Walls Could Talk* for HBO in the mid-nineties, she did it as a vehicle to speak out as a pro-choice crusader. And she very quietly has been a major benefactor of the Children's Craniofacial Association, even sitting in on a couple of operations during which children's distorted facial features were returned to their normal states.

The bottom line is that Cher has wits as sharp as her clothes and, frankly, her loyal legion of fans expect her to be entertaining well into her elder years. Will she be doing a remake of the "If I Could Turn Back Time" video in the famous "black dental floss" outfit created by Bob Mackie when she is eighty-seven? For Cher, who has a knack for always feeling and looking young, it's a distinct possibility. Who knows?

"There is always a new proposition with Cher. She's the 'original' Madonna in that she has been reinventing herself for decades," noted bestselling author J. Randy Taraborrelli (who wrote the 1986 unauthorized biography *Cher*) has said. "Just when we think she is finished, she comes back for more . . . and she's better than ever. I have a lot of respect for her because she understands that her true value is as an entertainer. She has always been entertaining, making it her life's work. Cher has never been dull, that's for sure."

Cher, of course is never just an actress or a singer or a fashionista or a social activist. She is a Renaissance woman who defies categorization, and that's what makes her, well, Cher.

Cher, of course is never just an actress or a singer or a fashionista or a social activist. She is a Renaissance woman who defies categorization, and that's what makes her, well, Cher.

CHAPTER TWO

Cherilyn Sarkisian LaPierre

When five-year-old Cherilyn walked out of a movie theater in 1951 with her mother, she knew she wanted to become famous one day. She didn't know exactly how, but the sounds of laughter and cheers coming from the people gazing at the big screen seemed like a good enough reason. How could anyone have possibly guessed that years later the dark-haired little girl would become one of the most revered entertainers of all time.

As a child, Cher was timid, yet, nonetheless, she yearned to be famous. "I used to go to the movies and thought what ever was in this dark room is what's happening." At age twelve, she started perfecting her autograph in preparation for being famous one day. "Shy and awkward," she confessed, "I lived in my dreams all day and all night—it was my secret fantasy. I knew I wanted to become a movie or television star. I couldn't think of anything else I could do. I really didn't think I could be a singer or dancer. I just thought I would be famous. That was my goal."

Cher was born Cherilyn Sarkisian on May 20, 1946, in El Centro, California. Her mother, Georgia Holt (formerly Jackie Jean Crouch), who was part Cherokee Indian, worked occasionally as an actress and model. She was a gorgeous blond with a genuine zeal for life. She came close to stardom only once, when she landed a part in the movie *The Asphalt Jungle*, but later lost out to another hard-working actress at the time: Marilyn Monroe.

"My mother was always working," recalls Cher. "She did a lot of things. She would do mod-eling and commercials and things like that. She even worked in an all-night diner, or something like that."

Growing up was hard on Cher and her younger half sister, Georgeanne. In fact, some of Cher's worst memories were of being so poor that she never had any pretty clothes to wear. "When you are poor, you feel inadequate. You think there is something wrong with you."

Cher admitted in the early seventies: "For a while we lived in Catholic charity houses. It was really hard for us. People didn't look down on us

Cher has said that when she was two years old, her mom said she used to run around the house naked all the time. Today, Cher quips, "Well, nothing has changed, except now I get paid for it!"

because I had bad clothes, but I always thought they could, and it bothered me." Cherilyn has many somber memories of her childhood, especially one in which her mother asked her six-year-old daughter, "How are we going to pay the rent?"

Perhaps what seemed to disturb young Cher even more were Georgia's constant, turbulent marriages and divorces. Upheaval was a way of life. Cher's mother presented her with four stepfathers, none of whom could offer any emotional or financial security. "I don't remember a man in the house. My mom was married eight times," Cher has said. "She married my father and left him. There was another man whom I don't remember because I was only two. Then my mother married my sister's father, John Southhall who is really the first man I remember." By Cher's fourteenth birthday, her mother married Gilbert LaPierre, a bank manager, who adopted the two sisters and offered them a better life, Cher went to a private school for the first time, even if it was only for a short while.

Mark Bego, author of the 2001 book *Cher If You Believe*, often drives through Cher's birthplace en route to his home in Phoenx, Arizona. He says every time he does, he smiles, thinking about how Cher is from El Centro and what it took for her to get to where she is today. "As I drive along the interstate freeway through the endless, dusty, agricultural fields of El Centro, I never fail to think: 'This is Cher's hometown!'" He offered, "It is sun-baked, flat, dull, and without distinction. It is everything Cher is not. However, it is amazingly inspiring to see, and to know that one of the most glamorous stars in the music and Hollywood realms, came from here. In my mind, it reinforces what Cher is all about: a talented woman who dared to dream of greatness and achieved it on her own terms."

Three of her mother's marriages were to Cher's father, John Sarkisian, a gambler and drug addict. Cher did not meet her father till she was eleven years old. "I didn't like him," she remembers. "He wasn't a nice person. I guess as a man he was okay, but not as a father. As a father he was weak. A father is someone who takes care of

It is believed that Sonny took this very early photo of Cher.

In the early sixties, Sonny Bono believed in Cher's talent and set out to make her a star the world would never forget.

you, and he couldn't even get himself together to do that."

As a teenager, Cher attempted to establish a relationship with her father, which only ended up being a disaster each time. The reconciliation was a painful disappointment for Cher. Her father's lifelong dependency on narcotics, among his many other problems, destroyed any possibility of Cher ever having any favorable sentiments toward him. "Man, he was such a letdown to me," she said. "I didn't have a father. He didn't take care of me like a father is supposed to do."

When John Sarkisian passed away in the mid-eighties, Cher reports that she ". . . didn't think about it. He was a junkie for so long. He pawned some of my mother's jewelry. Maybe if I had known him when I was younger, I might have liked him. I don't know."

With an interesting blending of French-English, Cherokee Indian, and Turkish-Armenian, her heritage has produced an intriguing, exotic beauty. But despite her long, jet-black hair, impossibly high cheekbones, and exotic appearance, Cher grew up thinking she was unattractive and and lacked talent, though all she had ever dreamed of was being famous. Everyone in Cher's family, except for her grandmother, was blond haired with light features. The first time Cher

"I lived in my dreams all day and all night—it was my secret fantasy. I knew I wanted to become a movie or television star. I couldn't think of anything else I could do."

Cher experienced dyslexia in school, but it never slowed down her aspirations to stardom. "It was a real problem for me." In the early sixties the learning disability was not as well publicized as it is today. As a child, Cher probably never dreamed she'd write a book someday.

office one too many times. "Cher was always doing something. She would never conform," Georgia Holt told a *Newsweek* reporter in 1987. "I was always being called into the principal's office."

One of those things Cher was doing at Montclair High, which enforced a strict dress code, was wearing flared, bell-bottomed jeans and midriff shirts, which she later became renowned for. "Cher could never fit into the dress code," the school's principal once commented. "She was different even in those days. She did sing and play in a trio and I remember them having good harmony."

In 1963, the sixteen-year-old girl moved in with a girlfriend in Los Angeles and supported herself at various jobs. Her twenty-seven-year-old next door neighbor was a music industry "gofer" named Salvatore ("Sonny") Bono. Bono worked with Phil Spector, the influential record producer responsible for creating the "wall of sound" for popular vocal acts of the day such as the Ronettes and the Righteous Brothers. Cher soon moved in with Bono, who informed her, "I don't find you particularly attractive and I have no designs on you. You keep the house clean and cook. I'll pay the rent." Cher, impressed by Bono's show-biz flair, turned her attention from acting to singing. Sonny Bono was the

saw her father she knew exactly where her dark looks had originated. "I wasn't even pretty," she recalled. "Georgeanne has this blond hair and green eyes like my mother, and I had this dark hair and brown eyes. When I saw my father walk through the house one day, I understood everything. I knew where I came from."

Discontented in school, Cherilyn LaPierre quit in the eleventh grade to study acting with renowned drama coach Jeff Corey. But not before her mother was called to the principal's one man who believed in Cher's talent and set out to prove it to the world.

Sonny and Cher Sing Backup on Spector Classics

In the early 1960s, Phil Spector would use whomever was hanging out at Gold Star Studios at the time. Sonny was working there; Cher was present whenever possible. Phil Spector employed Sonny Bono before he and Cher became Sonny & Cher. The duo often sang backup on many popular hit singles of the day. Cher, as longtime fans already know, rarely sang without Sonny because she was afraid to sing alone. Over the years, Sonny said that he sang on nearly every Phil Spector production, whether Cher sang backup with him or not. Cher says they sang backup on many songs, and to this day she can still pick her voice out on those early recordings.

Here is a list of songs from 1963 to 1965 believed to feature both Sonny and Cher as backup singers.

1963

"Da Doo Ron Ron (When He Walked Me Home)" by the Crystals

"Not Too Young To Get Married" by Bob B. Soxx and the Blue Jeans

"Then He Kissed Me" by the Crystals

"Be My Baby" by the Ronettes

"My Babe" by the Righteous Brothers

"A Fine, Fine Boy" by Darlene Love

"Baby, I Love You" by the Ronettes

"Christmas (Baby Please Come Home)" by Darlene Love

"Little Boy" by the Crystals

1964

"Hold Me Tight" by Treasures

"(The Best Part Of) Breakin' Up" by the Ronettes

"Do I Love You?" by the Ronettes

"All Grown Up Now" by the Crystals

"There's No Other Like My Baby/Not Too Young To Get Married" by the Crystals

"Yes Sir, That's My Baby" by Hale and the Hushabyes

"Walking in the Rain" by the Ronettes

"Christmas (Baby Please Come Home)" Darlene Love (second version of the song recorded)

"You've Lost That Lovin' Feeling" by the Righteous Brothers

"Bring Your Love to Me" by the Righteous Brothers

1965

"Born to Be Together" by the Ronettes

"Just Once in My Life" by the Righteous Brothers

"Is This What I Get for Loving You?" by the Ronettes

"Hung on You" by the Righteous Brothers

"Home of the Brave" by Bonnie and the Treasures

14

CHAPTER THREE

The Sixties:
We Got You, Babe

Hippies thought we were squares, squares thought we were hippies. —Cher

Cher first entered pop consciousness in the early sixties and Sonny Bono was the one man who could give her everything she desired. "When I first met Cher, she was sixteen and a waif," Bono recalled to *Song Hits* magazine. "On one hand she was a very mature kid, and on the other hand she was a naïve little girl. I told her she was going to be something great. I told her she was a flower that hadn't blossomed yet, but she would, and the whole world would know it."

As he encouraged her to sing, she eventually recorded the single," Ringo, I Love You" under the name of Bonnie Jo Mason. Sonny, the singer-songwriter and record promoter, had opened the door to a world of show-business possibilities for a teenage Cher as the couple originally billed themselves as "Caesar and Cleo," and played bowling

alleys and local clubs. In 1965, they switched to Sonny & Cher and hit gold with the Bono-penned "I Got You Babe," a sweet ode to married hippie life (though they didn't legally tie the knot until 1969 when Chastity was born). Within the next couple of years Sonny & Cher churned out a string of hit singles including "Baby Don't Go," "Just You," "But You're Mine," "What Now My Love," and "The Beat Goes On."

Subsequently, Cher had a solo career with just as many hits to match, including the Bob Dylan–written "All I Really Want to Do" and the Bono-penned "Bang Bang (My Baby Shot Me Down)," "You'd Better Sit Down, Kids," and "Where Do You Go?"

But it was their wild look—the love beads, long hair, striped, bell-bottomed jeans, and trademark fur vests that wowed fans all over the world. "It's a tough job being ridiculous, but if someone's

he Saturday Evening Post · April 23, 1966 · 35c

POST

Major report on the scandal of pollution
OUR DYING WATERS

How Hugh Hefner makes millions from the myth of
PLAYBOY'S BUNNIES

On the campaign trail with 'the candidate'
BOBBY KENNEDY

SONNY & CHÉR

In pop music
they're what's happening

got to do it, it might as well be me." Cher once said. "We were crazy dressers. We just looked bizarre next to other groups in beaded dresses and suits. We weren't accepted because of the way we looked. It's weird. People forget that it was the early sixties and we were still suffering from a bad case of Doris Day and Rock Hudson. Sonny and I were thrown out of every place you can imagine."

In 1965 Cher told teen magazine *Tiger Beat*: **I don't think I'm extravagant.** "I think Sonny is, but I think I am not because I'm not used to having money yet. I still look for bargains."

What Cher didn't know then is that she was on her way to becoming a cultural icon. She was deemed fashion's shock innovator—a role she has continued to play to a tee throughout her career.

Sonny became Cher's mentor. As Darlene Love once recalled: "Sonny was Cher's idol. Where he went, she followed. She was totally devoted to him and everyone knew it." From 1965 to 1967 Cher, both with Sonny and as a solo act, commanded the record charts. Not only were they pop idols, but millionaires, too. Together, they made appearances on various top, TV shows of the day, including *Shindig*, *American Bandstand*, *The Ed Sullivan Show*, and even touched on acting in an early episode from the *Man from U.N.C.L.E.* Prior to that was a pre–Sonny & Cher movie, titled *Wild on the Beach*, in which the couple performed a song on screen.

Sonny & Cher's Atco debut album *Look at Us*, sold over 600,000 copies in just three weeks.

Following Cher's "All I Really Want to Do" single, Sonny cut a single of his own titled "Laugh at Me," a youth-influenced record with a message. As the British invasion roared through America, Sonny & Cher headed overseas for a whirlwind, two-week promotional tour of Britain and were mobbed everywhere they appeared in public.

Following their initial success, the couple began to change from a teen singing team to a more mature act. Sonny told the press in 1967 that he and Cher wanted their music to be enjoyed by a wider audience, mainly adults. This new Sonny & Cher spoke out against drugs, which at the time was practically unheard of. In fact, it was the first time a top singing act had ever denounced narcotics. "To the hippies and drug culture, we kind of got taken along with the scene, even though we were not actually in it," Bono commented a couple years later. "When we did make a statement on drugs, and said we don't advocate them and it's stupid to get involved with them, we were out with the young."

The novelty of Sonny & Cher's singing hippie routine wore off and their pleasant pop folk-rock music was now being replaced by the psychedelic sounds of Jimi Hendrix, Cream, and the Beatles. Bono, undaunted by the duo's career setback, launched his wife in films by using his own money when studio financing was no longer available. But their movies, *Good Times* in 1967 and *Chastity* in 1969, were both box-office flops. The once hip husband-wife singing duo had fallen from grace with the youth culture.

In mid-1969, with a child to support and an enormous debt to the IRS, Sonny & Cher hit the nightclub circuit where they shed their former antiestablishment image and donned formal eveningwear, singing safe, middle-of-the road songs. This was also a prelude to Cher's future glamour-girl image and sexy sense of style that she would project in the coming decade. Despite the old adage that anyone who remembers the sixties wasn't there, Cher declared in 2002: "I didn't do drugs, so I can still recall everything. It was a great time, and we'll never recapture it."

Performing "The Beat Goes On" on a 1967 television show.

With Sonny, being interviewed for television.

CHAPTER FOUR

The Seventies: Cher—Superstar

Cher really came into her own in the seventies—personally and professionally. She had her own popular television show, split from longtime partner Sonny, had a second child, Elijah Blue Allman, and a huge string of hit, pop singles.

Then there's her influence on fashion at this point in time. Every week Cher would point her ultra-long, squared fingernails (she started that trend along with bringing "vamp" colored polish to the mainstream) and command the undivided attention of everyone watching. When television viewers across America watched Cher on the *Sonny & Cher Comedy Hour*, or later on the *Cher* show, they waited until the commercials to go to the kitchen for a snack because they didn't want to miss a minute.

Cher started out the seventies on an upswing. She and her husband and singing partner, Sonny, had their show until they divorced in 1974, but came back together as divorcees the following year. The once-devoted television audience didn't care much for the new *Sonny & Cher Show*, and it was canceled. Many serious Sonny & Cher fans of all ages were sincerely sad that the

> *"I went from pop diva to disco diva to what I really wanted to be at the time: a rock star. I found out later that I never really made it. I was still considered that glitzy lady on TV who did all the dramatic pop songs about love gone wrong."*

affection didn't mean as much and that Cher was pregnant by her new husband, rocker Gregg Allman, who proved to be more than a handful and whom she rarely saw.

Cher continued as a solo TV sensation until the late seventies, when she recorded one to two albums a year. She was distressed by the poor sales of some, including *3614 Jackson Highway*, a beautiful set recorded in Muscle Shoals, Alabama, with all the famous musicians who played on the sixties and seventies Stax soul hits. It was recorded in 1969 and released in 1970, before the *Sonny & Cher Comedy Hour* premiered on CBS. Many fans argue that is one of her finest forays on vinyl.

Mainstream members of the press argue that even though Cher scored big with her show and with hit singles like 1971's "Gypsies" and 1974's "Dark Lady," nothing spoke louder or garnered more attention than her impeccable fashions, created by Bob Mackie. Supposedly Cher met the designer while appearing on the *Carol Burnett Show* as a guest. Mackie was Burnett's exclusive television ensemble designer. Because of Cher's ultra-slim body shape which Mackie often described as "being so

Two rarely seen early-70s photos of Sonny & Cher

perfect, she didn't look lewd even if I left her nearly naked," the fashions were the most outrageous ever shown on the small screen and censors sometimes had a field day. When the *Sonny & Cher Comedy Hour* started up in 1971 as a summer replacement series on CBS, censors had to vote among themselves as to whether Cher could show her navel or not on prime-time TV. (Obviously, the vote went in favor of Cher's now trademark bellybutton). These days, the outfits the fans remember most are ones that showed off Cher's part–Native American heritage or "gypsy" side, especially the outfits with no sides. In fact, the *Sonny & Cher Comedy Hour* was the first show on which outfits so scant were allowed; it was said that allegedly barriers had been broken down by the late sixties' comedy show *Laugh-In*, which Cher guested on.

Cher and Elton John.

Cher's Children: Her Greatest Achievements

The only thing I really felt bad about is that I wasn't the mother I wanted to be. I was away too much. I did my best, but I have always felt you can't be in this business and be such a hot mother. I know my children know how much I love them even if I physically can't always be there with them. They are really the lights of my life. —**Cher**

Beyond the the public Cher lurks a sensitive woman and the mother of two: daughter Chastity and son Elijah. She's no different from any other mother who has hopes and fears and joys and tears for her children—and of course, a mother's unavoidable guilt. Cher has suffered many a heartbreak to become the mother she is today. For starters, before Chastity was born in 1969, Cher endured several devastating miscarriages that even today, are still too painful to talk about.

Chastity Bono

The only child of pop-icon couple Sonny and Cher will inevitably be remembered as the sweet, fair-haired little girl, smiling and giggling on stage with her parents. She was the quintessential child of celebrity—fashionably dressed, soon just as recognizable as her parents and the focal point of American television viewers' thoughts and their question of whether she would follow in her mother's footsteps.

Much to the public's dismay, and her parents, Chastity did not. She was hiding a secret from her family and the rest of world that would forever set her life on a different course. Chastity was gay and did not know how to tell her parents. Unfortunately, in 1990, she was outed by

Chastity, the sweet, smiling fair-haired little girl, did not follow in her famous mother's footsteps.

the tabloid *Star* and forced to deal with the issue in a very public and scrutinizing manner. Her famous parents had already been aware of her sexual orientation, and they were trying to deal with it within the confines of the family. The tabloid story made things for worse for Chastity especially, but also for Cher, who was already having a difficult time dealing with the news. Sonny, on the other hand, was immediately supportive, according to Chastity.

Cher and Chas.

In an effort to gain back some of the control she had lost due to the tabloid's report, Chastity publicly outed herself in April 1995, in *The Advocate*, a national gay and lesbian magazine for which she later became a freelance writer. Chastity received national recognition in 1995 for coming out, and later she interviewed her mother, Cher, in an acclaimed *Advocate* cover story.

From the day her coming-out issue hit the newsstands, Chastity became a sort of celebrity spokesperson for the gay and lesbian community.

She became a loud and clear voice for the Human Rights Campaign, a national lesbian and gay political organization, and was later named Entertainment Media Director for the Gay & Lesbian Alliance Against Defamation (GLAAD). In 1996, she traveled throughout the country as the National Coming Out Project spokesperson for the Human Rights Campaign, the nation's largest gay and lesbian political organization, addressing gay and lesbian groups on community issues and the importance of coming out.

Through these years, Cher and Chastity's relationship went from strained to stronger as they both worked through their feelings.

Chastity Sun Bono was born March 4, 1969. Her birth came at a difficult time for Sonny and Cher. The pop singing duo's popularity was beginning to wane and they were forced to go on the road to play small clubs and dinner theaters to pay the bills. Sonny was even known to borrow money from the chauffeur to get through the week. Cher has always despised this part of performing live because of the one-night gigs and shabby hotels they were forced to stay in. But as a new mother, she was happy not to be parted from her baby daughter.

At age two, little Chastity became a regular on the *Sonny & Cher Comedy Hour* as her famous parents brought the little girl out on stage every week to woo the television audience. "I don't remember much from my early years," Chastity has stated to the press. "As hard as it may be to believe, I barely remember my parents' television show or being brought on stage with them."

Chastity grew up in the spotlight along with her parents and eventually her half brother, Elijah Blue. Chas, as family and close friends affectionately call her, is an alumna of the High School for the Performing Arts, and she attended New York University's Tisch School of the Arts. She briefly ventured down the musical path, releasing the album *Hang Out Your Poetry* in 1993 with her band Ceremony on Geffen Records. However, despite her best efforts, nothing commercially substantial amounted from the band. A year later she served as a consultant for the television sitcom *Ellen*, starring Ellen DeGeneres, and appeared as a counselor in the episode in which Ellen's coming out was the topic.

In 1998, Chastity stepped down from her media-director post at GLADD to pursue creative entertainment projects and to prepare for a national promotional tour for her first book, *Family Outing* (Little Brown, 1998). *Family Outing* is a memoir of Chastity's experiences of coming out as a lesbian to her famous parents. Cher also tells her side of the story; relating all of the emotions attached to the situation including suspicion, denial, confrontation, and acceptance.

From as early as she can remember, Chastity Bono endured a constant struggle with herself and with her famous parents. In the years that have followed her coming out, Chastity has found new fame and Cher has reconnected with the daughter she has come to know. In summer 2002, Chastity's follow-up book, *An End to Innocence*, was published.

"My mom taught me you can do anything if you believe in yourself," she said. "Limitations are things to be overcome. There's nothing I want I can't get."

Sonny snapped this pic of big sister, Chastity, with baby brother, Elijah.

Elijah Blue Allman

Although Cher's marriage to her second husband, Gregg Allman, was short-lived, they did have a child together. Elijah Blue has managed to stay out of the celebrity spotlight for most of his life—until recently, as a member of the progressive goth-rock band Deadsy.

According to Elijah, the band's name comes from a David Anderson cartoon he saw in 1995 about a little dead kid. While Deadsy has not reached commercial fame and fortune, the band has acquired a strong following in Los Angeles and has garnered the attention of similar bands, landing a spot on *The Family Values Tour*.

As a member of Deadsy, Elijah goes by the pseudonym P. Exeter Blue I (or simply P. Exeter). He sings vocals and plays guitar. Each of the band's five members portrays a different "prep school" character in a twisted, narcissistic manner. "I'm very fascinated by Skull and Bones and secret societies and all that stuff that people are very curious about that create an air of mystique," Elijah, a former art student at Maine's Hyde School, told *Ray Gun* magazine in 1999. "That's consistent with what rock is about. I think that the best music-art is made when it has a stamp of who you are and your life and what you're about."

It was his prep-school environment that allowed the young musician to discover what most kids his age didn't have access to. "Being a kid of privilege, I often call this band 'a perversion of privilege.' I knew whatever I was going to do, it was going to be high-concept."

While Elijah may be hitting a stride and finding an identity with Deadsy, his musical roots undoubtedly begin with his famous parents. Born

July 10, 1976, Elijah has grown up in the music business, seeing the industry from all angles. Though Gregg Allman wasn't around, Cher exposed Elijah to many different musicians, namely her boyfriends. One musician in particular, Gene Simmons of Kiss, gave Elijah his first guitar when he was eleven, but it wasn't until much later that Elijah took a serious interest in music.

Elijah was a rebellious child, spending most of his formative years in boarding school. As the only child of Allman and Cher, Elijah had developed what he describes as: "my serious ownness to be able to survive in this world." It was while he was away at school in Maine that he met his future band mate Renn Hawkey (Dr. Nner). He fronted a couple of bands while in school and admits that he and his band mates at the time had all of the prep-school kids moshing. His Marilyn Manson–type singing, as well as the dark, gothic feel of his music, has made him the antithesis of what his parents used to be to their generation of music lovers. His parents were much loved by many in mainstream audiences, while he is much misunderstood.

Deadsy's latest release, *Commencement* from Sire records, has received decent, if not encouraging reviews. Korn's Jonathan Davis appears on the album—not too surprising since Deadsy is signed to Davis's Elemetree/ DreamWorks label. The band is working on its next CD, for which they will remix a few of the original tracks. The record is being coproduced by Josh Abraham (Limp Bizkit) and Jay Baumgardner (Papa Roach). Elijah admits that escaping the aura of his famous lineage is next to impossible, but he has used it to his advantage to get his foot in the door here and there or to just to receive those little "perks" to which celebrities are privy.

While Cher and Elijah have had their moments of both war and peace, Elijah had little to no contact with Gregg Allman while he was growing up, and that relationship is still strained. Cher obviously has influenced him more just by the way she's guided his life and the experiences she provided. Even though Cher's music has not

served as the influence for his venture into the business, Elijah has played guitar with Cher's band on her *Heart of Stone* tour in 1989 and also appeared on the soundtrack to the movie *A Walk on the Moon* with his mom for a smokin' rendition of the old Tommy James & the Shondell's classic "Crimson and Clover."

Elijah remains estranged, for the most part, from his famous father, but his relationship with Cher has grown ever stronger over the years. He remembers certain events in particular, like dressing up in her clothes when he was still a child, and getting ". . . into my mom's makeup." Mom even dressed him up as Bojangles once. "I always used to dress up in her clothes," Elijah said, "and play with her makeup and have it all Kisslike and stuff."

Today, Deadsy has a cult following. The goth-metal band may not be playing 20,000 seaters yet, but Mom, who doesn't always understand her son's music, does "dig it" and makes sure she attends any of P. Exeter I's Los Angeles club appearances. Cher's favorite Deadsy song? "Winners," because it is so beautiful.

Cher with twenty-two-year-old son Elijah, in 2001.

In Cher's love life in the seventies, she started going for bad-boy rockers. Her first serious post-Sonny affair was with music business impresario David Geffen, whom she admits had tremendous power, which was her main attraction to him—other than the fact he had some good ideas about the direction her musical career could take. In late 1974, she went from a short-lived affair with Alan Gorrie of AWB to Gregg Allman, whom she met at Hollywood's Troubadour during one of his concerts. He sent her a note via one of his road crew, and the rest was a train wreck waiting to happen—although it did produce a deep-voiced son who resembles his estranged father, plays guitar almost like his deceased uncle Duane, and who has toured with his mom in recent years.

The marriage, which included a lot of disappearances and drug binges by the goateed Mr. Allman, is something Cher has said she is glad she went through since Gregg was ultimately a sweet and sentimental fool underneath all his demonic episodes. Cher and Gregg even recorded the lukewarm *Allman & Woman* album in 1977, which sent Cher into a harder rock dimension musically for the remainder of the decade and into the eighties. When Cher signed with Geffen Records, she was suddenly a member of the corporate-rock arena, and had old-flame David Geffen directing her career and making sure she got all the primo hard rock material, although it often never got airplay because fans wanted the old Cher they knew from television and the Sonny & Cher days of the sixties.

75 CENTS

MARCH 17, 1975

TIME

®

GLAD RAGS TO RICHES

CHER

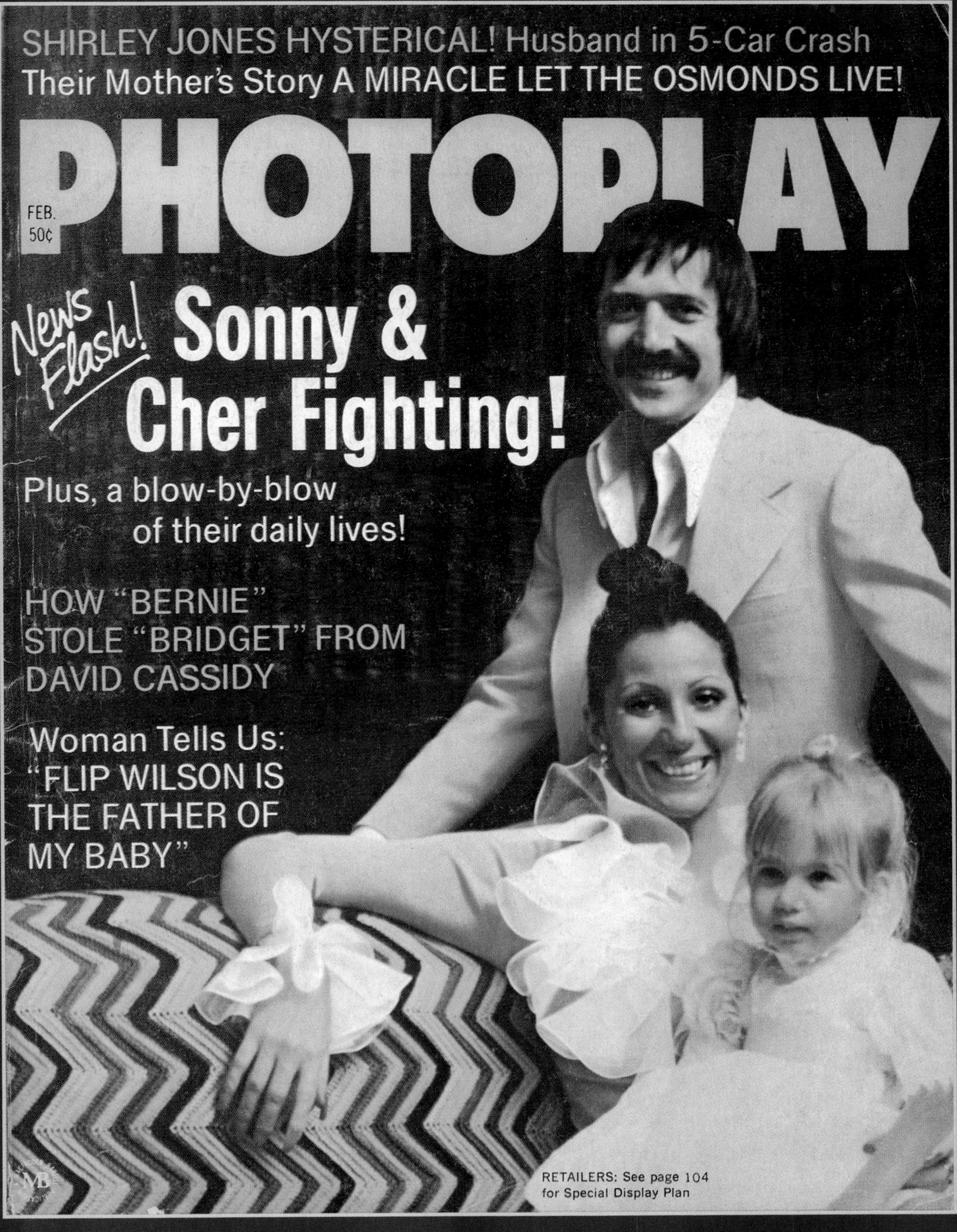

SHIRLEY JONES HYSTERICAL! Husband in 5-Car Crash

Their Mother's Story A MIRACLE LET THE OSMONDS LIVE!

PHOTOPLAY

FEB.
50¢

News Flash!

Sonny & Cher Fighting!

Plus, a blow-by-blow
of their daily lives!

HOW "BERNIE"
STOLE "BRIDGET" FROM
DAVID CASSIDY

Woman Tells Us:
"FLIP WILSON IS
THE FATHER OF
MY BABY"

Solo Cher from her 1975 show.

On the most personal of levels, Cher admits that the seventies were a time of reawakening and spiritual growth for her because she always had Sonny to take care of every facet of her life. She just had to go onstage or into the studio and perform. That was pretty much all that was required of her. She did not know how to write a check or even how to order food in a restaurant.

Cher admits that she fell in love with being a single mother in the seventies and started a side business, which she kept under her hat: renovating mansions in Los Angeles's tonier neighborhoods and selling them at a profit. It was reported that she "fixed up" anywhere from a dozen to twenty homes. For most of her post-Sonny seventies days, she lived in a Bel Air home decorated in ancient Egyptian style because, supposedly, a psychic told Cher she was a member of Egyptian royalty in ancient times. Cher's love of this style later emerged when picking out items to sell in her mail-order catalog, *Sanctuary*.

Eventually, Cher moved out to Malibu because she was tired of the stuffiness of the Beverly Hills–Bel Air area and decided she could be more at peace with oceanfront property. She has remodeled and sold several Malibu homes and continues to do so today.

Cher ended the sensational seventies as a completely different woman from when she began the decade. She was a little embarrassed by her brief stint as a roller disco and dance artist. Fans remember how she was constantly photographed by paparazzi at Studio 54 and other hotspots of the era. It was the drama of her years in this decade that helped create the celebrity, Cher persona.

Looking back, J. Randy Taraborrelli sums it up like this: "The Sonny & Cher TV shows . . . and the scandal with Greg Allman, being pregnant with his kid and on TV with Sonny for that final season." What fun. Who would do that!!!??? Only Cher. Bob Mackie, all of those great 'armpit' outfits, the belly-button foolishness, the ramp she

used to run down at the beginning of the *Cher* show, her awkward monologues, Laverne . . . Tina Turner . . . Elton . . . Michael Jackson . . . what great years."

Cher once told an interviewer how she felt at the end of the famed "Me Decade": "I was happy the seventies were over. It was undoubtedly the most turbulent part of my life. I had a baby, I ended two marriages, and found out what it was like to be truly independent. It was hard, even though I had plenty of money, and I just wondered how people with less means and support from loving people than me got through it. I finally felt like a woman. I also changed musical direction. I went from pop diva to disco diva to what I really wanted to be at the time: a rock star. I found out later that I never really made it. I was still considered that glitzy lady on TV who did all the dramatic pop songs about love gone wrong. But I did my best to become the person I wanted to be at the time, both spiritually and physically, and I think I did a damn good job if I say so myself."

While Cher was not getting offered any of the movie roles she had pined for since she was a high schooler in the San Fernando Valley, she made a huge impact as a comedienne, pop chanteuse, and fashion plate. Television viewers from eight to eighty-eight tuned in to watch the seventies superstar week after week.

The Eighties: Unmasked on the Big Screen

There was never any question: Cher had wanted to be an actress since she was sixteen years old, and she told Sonny Bono on one of their initial meetings that that was the main goal in her life plan. Sonny said he'd help her with her acting goals. But it wasn't until 1969, when the hit-making couple pawned all their earthly possessions except their car to put together the cash to produce the clunky, runaway adventure *Chastity*, that Cher got to experience what it was like to be a real movie star. Sure, the hippie-pop duo did the musical comedy *Good Times* back in 1967, but Cher was required mainly to sing and Sonny and Cher basically played themselves.

So you can imagine what it was like for Cher in 1980 when director Francis Ford Coppola came backstage at one of her Caesar's Palace shows in Las Vegas and said, "You're so good. Why aren't you doing movies?" Cher has since commented on that event to the press by stating: "I'd been trying to get a job in movies since Elijah was born, and now he was five years old. It wasn't that people didn't know me. I hung out with Jack Nicholson and Anjelica Huston and Warren Beatty. I went to directors and producers in New York and California and I couldn't get arrested."

Cher admits that her fear at the time was that directors considered her "too old or too tall or too ethnic." After guesting on a television special with Shelley Winters, the veteran actress told Cher if she was "serious" about acting, she should go to New York. Cher was thirty-five at the time, and

Cher was undoubtedly at the top of her game in the late 1980s. Having won several awards, she could write her own ticket in Hollywood—and she did!

The decade began with her Broadway debut in *Come Back to the 5 & Dime, Jimmy Dean, Jimmy Dean*, and by early 1988 she was holding the elusive Oscar like the lifetime-achievement triumph it was!

dialed, said to Mr. Altman, "Is Cher there?" To which he replied, "What the hell would Cher be doing here?" When Cher's mom realized what had just happened, she laughed and mentioned Cher was now living in New York. Altman asked how he could reach Cher for a play he was holding auditions for called *Come Back to the 5 & Dime, Jimmy Dean, Jimmy Dean*. The rest, as they say, is both Broadway and movie history.

Cher went over to Altman's luxurious apartment on Central Park South and found future costars Kathy Bates, Sandy Dennis, and Karen Black sitting on the floor. She felt out of place, especially portraying the transvestite Joe, and

Cher's success as an actress was not just about getting awards or even getting offered "important" roles.

more than ready to get off the Vegas circuit. So she moved into a spacious loft above Tower Records in Greenwich Village, where Keith Richards became one of her neighbors. Her first audition was for Joseph Papp of the famous Joe Papp Public Theater productions, also in the Village on lower Broadway.

This audition wouldn't lead anywhere, but fate had something special in store for Cher shortly thereafter. One day, Cher's mom accidentally speed-dialed her old friend Kathryn Altman and woke up her famous director-husband, Robert. Holt, unaware of whom she had just

The 1980s brought us Cher, the movie star. She finally began to achieve her ultimate goal as a screen siren.

How Cher Prepares for a Scene

"I've never studied acting," admitted Cher in 1984, following the release of *Mask* (though she purposively did in 1964 with famed acting coach, Jeff Corey). "I still might at some point. But I find for me, I just have to go out there and do it."

Over the years, Cher has learned how to integrate her musical and onstage experience into her work as a dramatic actress. Though she views performing live-in-concert and acting as two completely separate experiences, she has made connection between them that cannot be ignored.

"Music is more real to me than words," Cher revealed. "A song can evoke emotion. It's unconscious." While she was filming *Mask*, Cher recalled listening to cassette tapes of songs like "Every Breath You Take" by the Police, "Skylark" by Aretha Franklin, and ". . . And I'm Tellin' You I'm Not Goin'" by Jennifer Holiday, through headphones. By the time she would be called onto the set, she'd discovered that the music allowed her the ability to find the right mood to get into the scene.

Because her tough character, Rusty Dennis, experiences a wide range of emotions throughout the film, Cher discovered that music could help her achieve the right state of mind to evoke a particular emotion. "Doing this part has been a wonderful experi-ence for me as an actress, but torturous on me as Cher," she revealed. "After doing five days during the week, I find that about Wednesday it really starts to get to me and it's not until Saturday and Sunday that I find myself again. Then it's time to get back into it again the next day."

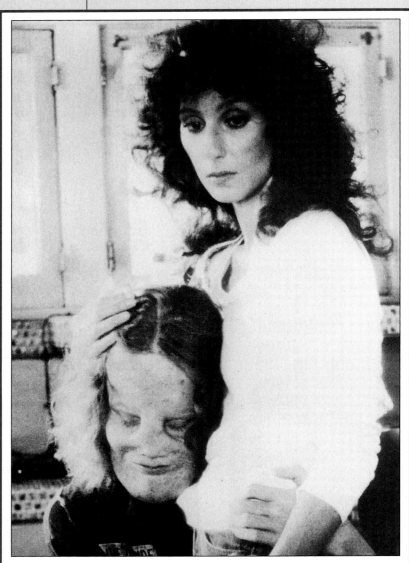

In *Mask*, Cher's character, Rusty Dennis, experiences a wide range of emotions. Cher learned that listening to certain types of music helped her achieve the right mood she needed to complete the scene.

In Atlantic City, 1981.

nowadays, says her audition was a "disaster." But Altman kept her in mind for the character of Sissy, and shortly thereafter, she scored the role. Cher joined Actor's Equity, and started on the role of Sissy, getting Elizabeth Taylor's old dressing room at the Martin Beck Theater. The play opened on February 18, 1982.

Reviews were not gracious, but one famous director snuck into a Wednesday matinee: Mike Nichols. He offered Cher a leading part in *Silkwood* opposite Meryl Streep. At first, Cher was apprehensive about playing opposite such a legendary actress, but when Cher and Streep met at Nichols's production office, they immediately hugged.

Filming went smoothly except for one scene in which Cher's character had to eat an Entenmann's chocolate-covered doughnut. This required two dozen takes and she really had to eat a whole doughnut each time, but Cher thoroughly enjoyed playing Dolly Pelliker, a composite of Karen Silkwood's sister and Karen's friend. Cher earned an Oscar nomination for her role, something that restored her pride and gave her hope that she would now be considered for leading roles.

Next up on the agenda was *Mask*, directed by Peter Bogdanovich (whom Cher actually met for the first time back in 1966 when he was a journalist interviewing Sonny and Cher for the *Saturday Evening Post*). Cher loved playing Rocky's biker chick mom, and loved having macho actor Sam Elliott play her boyfriend. Cher won Best Actress

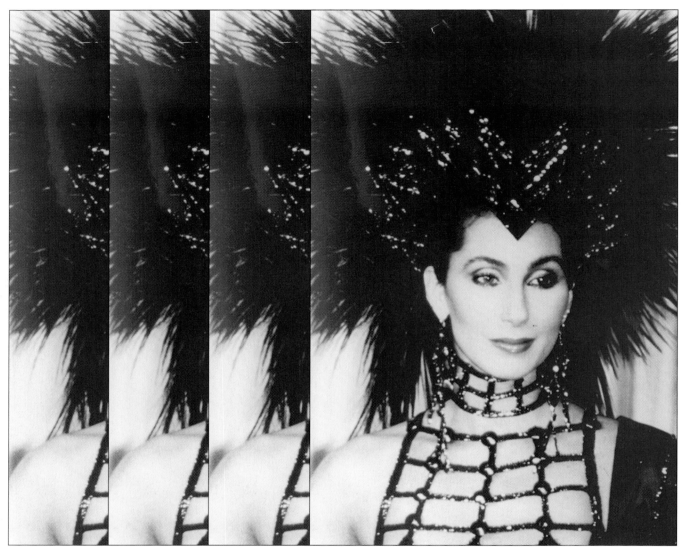

Presenter Cher shows the Academy that she knows how to dress for the occasion.

at the Cannes Film Festival that year, but was apparently dismayed by rumors that she was dating Eric Stolz, who played Rocky, a real-life teen afflicted with craniofacial disease. (Cher was actually dating Josh Donen at the time.)

Hollywood insiders told Cher she would probably be nominated for an Academy Award, but it turned out to not be so. Still, she went to the Oscars and blew the house down in a black, sequined Bob Mackie outfit with headdress. Cher asked her longtime designer to do a Mohawk Indian–looking number for her, and some would say he carried the concept just a little too far! Even David Letterman commented it would have "been suitable to wear for Darth Vader's funeral."

It was also during this same time frame that she called Letterman an "a-hole" on national television for not paying her pre-agreed-to $38,000 hotel bill at Morgan's Hotel when she appeared on his late-night show. Cher later apologized.

Next up on her acting agenda was *The Witches of Eastwick*, costarring Jack Nicholson, Michelle Pfeiffer, and Susan Sarandon. Cher was hurt when George Miller told her that Nicholson thought Cher was "not sexy enough" to play one of his character's love interests. When Cher heard this for the first time, it was her birthday and she cried as her sister, kids, and best friend Paulette Betts brought her a cake and sang in her suite at—you guessed it—the Morgan Hotel.

Belting out the hits for the faithful in Las Vegas.

Cher later found out that it wasn't Nicholson, but Miller, who didn't want her in his new movie. But issues were put aside, and Cher went to work dealing with the difficult director (who carried around a chalkboard writing cryptic notes to himself all day long). The movie turned out to be a blockbuster, but due to nervousness and occasional boredom from too much "hurry up and wait," Cher sat in dressing trailers with her costars and ate Reese's Pieces and other junk food by the bag. Soon, her weight had ballooned up to 125 pounds, although that is hardly heavy considering her five-foot-seven stature.

Cher started doing the New York club scene, although at the time she felt it was meant for "kids," and she wanted to go back to Los Angeles. But one night at the now-defunct Heartbreak, she met handsome, hunky, twenty-two-year-old Rob Camilletti. They soon began watching movie marathons together and dancing. Cher had just turned forty, so there was an eighteen-year age gap between them; the press had a field day.

It was apropos that Cher had started dating a *young* "Italian Stallion," as she was just starting work on *Moonstruck*, a film about an over-emotional Italian-American family in Brooklyn. Nicholas Cage might have played Cher's love interest Ronnie Cammareri in *Moonstruck*, but the young Rob was her real-life Ronnie.

Cher won a Best Actress Oscar that year, and admits she was as surprised as anyone. Of course, even though she won, viewers were talking more about her outrageous Bob Mackie gown than her award the next morning. The black-beaded number was much more subdued and cosmopolitan looking then the one she'd worn the year she was nominated for *Mask*, however.

In February 1988, Cher had another run-in with David Letterman, who apparently did not give her any problems about her hotel bill this time, but who gave her another kind of stress—he pressured her to sing "I Got You Babe" on camera with ex-husband Sonny. It would be the first time in over a decade that they had sung it together. Since the crowd started cheering and

whistling, Cher couldn't help but oblige, but her displeasure was thinly veiled. Chastity and Sonny's current wife, Mary, were crying in a booth at the side of the stage, and several members of the audience had tears in their eyes. The ever-the-pro Cher simply held herself together and performed. However, it would be a long time before she would appear on *Late Night with David Letterman* again.

In early 1988, Cher was undoubtedly at the top of her game. Her Academy Award win meant she could write her own ticket in Hollywood. In 1989, she was offered a role in the comedy *Mermaids*, opposite Winona Ryder, then the hottest young actress in movieland, and recent Oscar-winner Bob Hoskins. The film was released in 1990, and made lukewarm profits at the box office, but her remake of Betty Everett's "Shoop Shoop" song, which was a moderate hit in the U.S., was a big hit in Europe.

By the end of the decade, Cher, the award-winning actress, was much in demand. But it would be awhile before she'd star in another major film.

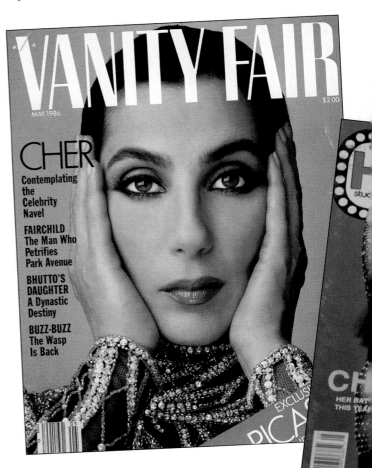

THE BUDGET COMPROMISE
Will Wall Street Buy the Deal?

Newsweek

Cher

Movie Star,
Video Vamp—
and All Business

Super Bowl's
Joe Theismann
Swing to *The
Curly Shuffle*
Did Diana Ross
kin NYC?

working mom on location

People
weekly
JANUARY 23, 1984

Cher
She's gay and
gritty in *Silkwood*,
but offscreen she
still loves glamour

New Woman
FEBRUARY 1988 $1.95

How to Know
When He's
the Right Man
And It's the
Right Time to
Fall in Love

**STRESS
AND YOUR
STARS**
Special Horoscope
to Help You

10 Keys

Designer Chic on the New

HORROR
Turning B
bucks, H
grosses out

us

The New
CHER
She's got
and a
as ro

Rest in peace,
Disney: An old
farewell
Edith Bu...

A new
secretar...

Björn
record
love games
on and off

Lynda Carter
inside her

TV HOST
Weekly
JUNE 28 to JUL 4
LEHIGH VALLEY CABLE EDITION 03

IN J
CHE
give
accla
perfor

MAS

New Yo

Finally—Light at the End of

**Cher
And
Altman**

People
weekly
JANUARY 25, 1988 $1.69

What Happened to Sam Cohn? • 'Memphis Belle' • Video: Radio

PREMIERE
NOVEMBER 1990
Movie
Magazine

HARRIS: PRAYING
A STATE OF GRACE

UP KAUFMAN
HES THE
TED ENVELOPE

IE FISHER ON
DRUGS, AND
CARDS FROM
EDGE'

E DISNEY:
THEY'VE GOT,
THEY WANT,
THEY'LL GET IT

WINONA & CHER
TWO FISH OUT OF WATER IN 'ME
BY CHRISTOPHER CONNELLY

Special Section: Our 1987 Wrap Party • The Fall of David Puttnam • The Best of

PREMIERE
FEBRUARY 1988
Movie
Magazine

**CHER,
SERIOUSLY**
SHE SIZZLES WITH NICOLAS
CAGE IN 'MOONSTRUCK'

SHOT BY SHOT:
HOW TO FILM A
NUDE SCENE

ate
woman
ER

e
k
her
&

ay:
me
ou'

OLLECTORS

ollywood
Magazine
FOR NOSTALGIA FILM & VIDEO COLLECTORS

Then and

FREE!
CAROLE LOMBARD
RARE COLOR POSTER

THE SEX DRIVE
Hank Williams Jr. lives
up to his C&W legacy
Outtasight! An L.A.
orthodontist invents
invisible braces
The brave nun who
preached to the Pope

CHER
She and
KISS's
GENE SIMMONS
bare their
life together
and marriage
thoughts
for the
first time

HER LIF

BETTE DA
THE MEN THEY SH

Where To Buy
How To Sell

Should kids see *Kindergarten Cop*?

People
weekly
JANUARY 21, 1991 $1.95

**EXCLUSIVE!
CHER**

Superfit at 44,
the *MERMAIDS* star
says in a new
book that her secret
is a healthy life
(and not the surgeon's
knife): "I'd like to
look really great for
as long as I can.
Anything else? She'd
have another ba
in a heartbeat

CHAPTER SIX

The Unmistakable Cher Style

Change is a constant rage for glamour-woman Cher. Through the decades, her unique look has sparked nearly as much curiosity as her love life—well almost. So, she's a clotheshorse supreme who will wear anything that pleases her, and tough on the fashion critics who laugh at her. Age is not taken into consideration. And if Cher wants to wear overalls with a leather jacket, she will; if she wants to show off the glitziest of Bob Mackie gowns, she will.

Cher might be the only celebrity who does "biker" as well as she does "diva," and one of her

"Top-notch designers like Anna Sui, Tom Ford, and Dolce & Gabbana call Cher an inspiration."

live shows (with all its costume changes) lets you get a little bit of each flavor. There are not many celebrities that manage to look so stylish in so many different ways. Also, so few have presented their public personas with such remarkable drama and flair. Cher stands alone in a supreme circle as one superstar who has accomplished it with a free-spirited sense of fun.

Cher inherits her striking, trademark, high cheekbones from her Cherokee mother's side of the family, and her deep, soulful brown eyes from her Armenian father. Her luxurious black hair is attributed to both parents. Her interesting take on makeup and beauty only accentuates the drama of her ensembles. Cher loves to experiment with the latest makeup looks, and over the years, only one cosmetic rule has applied: make the eyelashes look as long, lush, and black as possible.

The Sixties

When sixteen-year-old Cherilyn met Sonny Bono, she was just starting to experiment with makeup, and dressed in basic blue jeans and casual shirts. In fact, a friend once commented after the couple became famous in 1965 that Cher often "used to pick up the same jeans off the floor from the night before and put them back on." But once she became a national singing star, Cher was the queen of hip huggers, crop tops, and fur vests (at the urging of Sonny). As a matter of fact, the fur vests often got them thrown out of conservative

On designing this famous Cher Oscar gown, Bob Mackie stated, "It was just like assembling a Rose Parade float."

Sonny's outfits, many of which had drawstring fronts (called "Tom Jones" shirts at the time) complemented Cher's in terms of colors and level of dressiness. Both Sonny and Cher favored Beatle-type boots in all colors, not to mention the occasional fur "chukka boots" when the weather permitted it.

Cher's sixties makeup was natural-looking except for the Cleopatra eyes and white or light pink frosted lipstick she often sported. She apparently wore little or no blush at the time, and usually had on clear nail polish. Jewelry was kept at a minimum except for three or four large, semiprecious stone rings she flashed on her fingers. Cher loved to collect rings at that time, and at performances, fans often hurdled rings on stage for her. Cher's hair was usually long and straight with bangs. She often ironed it and trimmed the ends herself. Teenage girls, enamored of her fashionable hip, beatnik appearance, emulated the

One of the many costume changes from the *Heart of Stone* tour.

hotels and restaurants, although she and Sonny were real "straight-arrow" types who never touched drugs or partook in any of the usual rock 'n' roll debauchery.

Cher also used to pass time on the road by sketching outfits she'd like to wear onstage. She then took these to a Hollywood tailor to have them made up. Cher had a perfectly flat belly that was rarely covered, and she often favored flowered cotton prints, bright-colored hip-hugger jeans, and wide belts. Unlike her later years, the young Cher mainly favored comfortable, casual clothing, although some of her bell-bottom outfits, especially the flowered "elephant bells" she wore at Sonny & Cher's headlining Hollywood Bowl show, were flashier than what a non–rock star would wear, and were distinctively Cher.

"The hat came first," says Bob Mackie of this 1998 Oscar creation for Cher. He modeled it after one Cher had seen in the film *Out of Africa*. "The dress was almost like a 1915 dress, and the hat was very typical of that time. I don't know why everyone was so horrified by it!"

clients like Judy Garland, who had more figure flaws, he created very covered-up, monochromatic numbers; but with Cher, it was just the opposite. Bob Mackie also took advantage of Cher's desire to show off her part–Native American heritage—thus the exotic Native-American flavored sequined numbers with headdresses that he designed for her.

There seemed to be no end to Mackie and Cher's collective excesses. Week after week, the

(text continued on page 53)

pop/rock singing star. This was Cher's first taste of being a role model, a label that would transform itself many times over and carry Cher through for years to come.

The Seventies

Cher created a whole new look for young, affluent America in the 1970s, thanks to the creative costuming of Bob Mackie, a veteran designer for many top television and Broadway shows. He wasn't afraid to put thousands of sequins on Cher and get her into floor-length gowns—something she had never worn before and which she had considered to be for society matrons or bridesmaids.

Mackie took advantage of Cher's great physical attributes, including her long legs, flat stomach, and his favorite, her "great armpits," and created sleeveless gowns with bare midriffs and slits up the sides. Mackie always said that Cher was the easiest body he ever had to dress. For

Cher's passion for fashion.

Wigging Out!

Cher's love affair with wigs goes back to the early seventies, when she started on the *Sonny & Cher Comedy Hour*. Her hair was beginning to suffer damage from constant styling and restyling for song spotlights and skits, and the hair personnel on the show decided to invest a thousand dollars and upward in customized human-hair wigs. The most-used wig was a three-thousand-dollar replica of her then ultra-long black locks. Having wig changes also allowed Cher instant hair-color changes. Custom wigs were also created for certain characters on the show, the most popular being the red forties style updo worn by the tacky but lovable "Laverne."

Later, on Cher's solo show, she really let lose with wigs of all different textures, including super-frizzy and crimped looks that were popular back then. She even had wigs that were made outrageously long for certain vamp numbers that she did, including one twelve-foot wig that was tied to her natural hair and then to a tree. This is pictured in her book *The First Time* and was also seen in a 2000 Bob Mackie fashion display in New York City.

Although wigs lost their popularity with the general public in the mid-seventies, Cher has continued wearing them to the present day. In the eighties, she (along with Tina Turner) helped popularize the fright wig. Cher was even seen in a purple wig, which she wore to accent a red-and-black ensemble. Her most famous wig of the eighties was the three-foot-high, black, ultra-fright wig she wore to the Oscars in 1986. When she accepted her own Oscar in 1988, she wore a more subtle, curly, upsweep type of wig that blended easily with her natural hair color. She also had some ultra-wavy, "natural-looking" styles made for live shows in the eighties.

Cher's present Malibu mansion has a special, climate-controlled wig room that sports reportedly close to one hundred hairpieces of every conceivable length, style, and color—many of which Cher takes on the road with her for a quick-change look. She says she styles them herself, but she has two stylists always on call to come over and prepare wigs for big events.

One of Cher's most popular wig styles of the nineties was a chin-length bob cut she had made in nearly every color from pink to blond and back again, and it was considered one of her most conservative 'dos ever. Another was a ravishing redhead look that was made in a couple of different styles and lengths.

The years 2000–2001 have been sprinkled with Cher in mainly straight, shoulder-length styles with bangs, although a late 2001 public appearance (at the *Harry Potter* movie premiere in London) showed her going long, wavy, and golden blond. No one was sure if she was trying to emulate Lady Godiva or Mary Pickford, but it certainly was a unique ultra-retro look that only someone as glamorous and quirky as Cher could get away with! As a critic from *The New York Times* once noted, "When you take away those wild wigs, there's an honest, complex screen presence underneath."

One of Cher's favorite places to shop for wigs is at an exclusive wig-making facility in London. On one big shopping spree, a London newspaper reported that Cher had dropped a cool $4,000 on new hairpieces. Who, but Cher could be so hardcore when it comes to hair?

viewers tuned in to see what America's hottest female TV star was wearing. Then came the major upheaval when Cher showed her navel on national television in one of Mackie's more daring creations—a forerunner to the new millennium's low-cut jeans. "What's more innocent than a navel?" Mackie has said. "It was a beautiful navel and a beautiful torso. The thing about Cher was that however little she wore, she never looked vulgar because nothing ever hung over. She was like a coat hanger. It was much like dressing a Barbie doll, except that she was life-size and sang and danced. Cher could wear anything."

When disco came into popularity in the late seventies, Cher stood up and took notice. She was not only part of the roller-disco craze, but also took part in the reinterest in 1940s styles, which included severe shoulder pads and button earrings. Her makeup appeared heavy and included, square, bird-claw nails and lips in deep red or "vamp" colors.

The Eighties

Cher's look in the eighties was very rock 'n' roll, probably influenced by the young musicians she had been taking up with since the late seventies. She was influenced by the heavy metal glam era, and was often seen sporting studded belts, thigh-high, black-leather boots, shoulder-duster earrings and colored streaks in her hair. She also started getting into wilder, messier hairstyles—which were mainly wigs—while onstage.

For part of the early eighties, she had an ultra-short, spiky, punk do. Fans chuckled that while Cher, the mother, was looking wilder than ever, Chastity, the daughter, stuck with the preppy, button-down cotton shirt, chinos, and docksider look. But in the middle of all this rock-and-roll gear sporting, Cher still wore the classic, outrageous, beaded Mackie gowns to both the Golden Globes and Oscars.

Cosmetically speaking, Cher gave up the squared, long nails, but started sporting peacock eye makeup. The nonglamorous side of Cher came out in both *Silkwood* and *Mask*. In both films, she did scenes with minimal makeup and wore no-nonsense attire. Sometimes off camera, she was spotted in warm, cozy sweaters with fuzzy slippers, which were considered out of character.

Lucky fans, at this time, could purchase Cher's castoffs for a song at Susie Coehlo's *A Star Is Worn* boutique on Melrose Avenue, which unfortunately only lasted a few years. Still, Cher, the ultimate trendsetter, every year of the decade cast a new look, which was happily copied by thousands of women everywhere.

The Nineties

Cher, as expected, was everywhere in terms of fashion looks in the 1990s. A lot of admirers like to remember her ultra-bare ensemble in the "If I Could Turn Back Time" video, which was shot on the USS *Intrepid* in New York City with thousands of real-life sailors gleefully looking on. That's the Cher that female impersonators most like to take on, but our favorite diva actually went into a more conservative period in the nineties, sporting trendy but less elaborate blazers and black pants when caught in public.

Some of Cher's greatest shopping sprees were done at this time. Always being a clotheshorse, Cher was spotted shopping in both famous and unknown boutiques on both coasts, including those of small designers out of Soho and Melrose Avenue. But just as commonly, fans would catch her coming out of the expensive Bennis-Edwards, Otto Tootsi Plohound, and Manolo Blahnik.

Her shoe collection was said to number over six hundred pairs at one point in the mid-nineties, but Cher did regular pairing down for charity, and seemed not to wear the same pair of shoes more than a few times.

Also, during the 1990s, Cher picked up a love for goth style, thanks perhaps to mysterious rockers like Marilyn Manson who were popular at the time. Cher was seen in lots of leather and interesting jewelry with crosses and Egyptian motifs. Cher also became popular for her interesting off-the-shoulder shirts and other clingy numbers with oddly shaped straps.

Bob Mackie: The Man Behind the Glam

He's the guy who revved up Cher's wardrobe back in 1970 (then called "the rich hippie look"), and ever since, the divine diva has used him to keep her stage look glamorous and mysterious.

"Glamour," "drama," and "sirens" are the words floating around behind the scenes of any Bob Mackie fashion show. His fall 2001 collection, which the editors of this book caught in New York's Bryant Park, was dubbed "Foreign Intrigue." The good ol' Mackie glitz was on, full-steam-ahead, as leggy models strutted their stuff on the catwalk in sequined versions of Turkish harem outfits and Asian geisha gear.

Bob Mackie was born Robert Gordon Mackie in Monterey Park, California, on March 24, 1940. He studied advertising and illustration at Pasadena City College 1957–58, then costume design at Chouinard Art Institute at Los Angeles, California. Mackie's background as a designer started in the movies and television.

Mackie is best known for designing the clothes and gowns for Cher, whom he has "dressed" since the early seventies. Mackie also designed costumes for Carol Burnett in the *Carol Burnett Show* 1967–78. In this weekly variety show, Mackie exhibited his true genius as an interpretative designer; Mackie's costume designs led the audience to the character being portrayed, and not the personality of the actor.

In 1979, he wrote *Dressing for Glamour*. In it, he said "Glamour is a state of mind, a feeling of self-confidence." He admitted that his original love of fashion came from watching movies when he was growing up in the fifties, and that one of his role models was famed studio fashion designer Edith Head. This fifties influence is still evident in his work, especially in his sequined halter gowns, reminiscent of movie queen Marilyn Monroe's heyday.

Occasionally a bit of Joan Crawford pops up in his creations with heavily padded shoulders. Many of these were worn by Cher back in the days of the *Sonny & Cher Comedy Hour* and on her solo show.

In the seventies, a *Newsweek* television critic commented about Mackie's television show costumes: "The real star is a cool, hip, certifiably freaky costume designer named Bob Mackie. Television hasn't shown so much glitter and flesh since NBC did a special on Liberace's closet." For young American women of that era, trapped in faded bell-bottomed jeans and tie-dyed T-shirts, the show was a dazzling dance of exuberant possibilities. "Suddenly, every young girl in the whole world had her hair parted down the middle, hanging straight down, whether she looked good in it or not," Mackie commented on the show's extraordinary influence. "Now that was scary."

What about his extraordinary influence working in television? Since the seventies, Mackie has won an astonishing seven Emmys and has been nominated thirty times. But fans and fashion critics alike would be the first to admit it was the 1975 *Cher and Other Fantasies* television special, which featured musical guest stars Elton John and Bette Midler, as his most unforgettable television work.

This also proved to be the beginning of a long collaboration with Elton—"the female Cher"—whose trademark flamboyant concert costumes like Donald Duck and Minnie Mouse were Mackie's creations. "He was always lovely to work with, although I think he may have been loaded most of the time back then," says Mackie. "We'd show him ten sketches and he'd order twelve. He's always loved dressing up and loved to make an entrance and get lots of attention. The only restriction was he needed to be able to sit at the piano."

In 1982, Bob Mackie turned to ready-to-wear and established Bob Mackie Originals. He already had a ready-made clientele: women who had watched him dress Cher and Carol Burnett, and who watched other television variety-hour shows like *The Judy Garland Show* and *The King Family Show*. But, Mackie did not stop his creative genius with the *Bob Mackie Originals*. He started designing clothes for the designer Barbie series by Mattel. These are appropriately called *Bob Mackie Dolls* and are sold everywhere, including traditional retail stores, catalogs, and online shops. They are highly collectible and garner hefty bids on eBay and other online auctions every week.

You can read plenty about Bob Mackie and the mutual admiration society he shares with Cher in her 1999 book *The First Time* or in his 2000 *Unmistakably Mackie*.

In 2001, *People* magazine chose Cher as one of the "Fifty Greatest Style Setters" and Mackie was picked as one of the Top Ten "Classic Designers to the Stars." Mackie himself is quite the fashion plate, always looking like the distinguished older man, wearing fine, natural fabrics such as cashmere and camel hair. He is a little flashier than most men his age, but he's got as much style as the famous women he dresses! —Anne M. Raso

Cher helped Bob Mackie create the classic tacky Laverne look.

Mackie knows the secret to maintaining Cher. Here is a selection of famous Cher gowns by Mackie.

55

Cher on Cosmetic Surgery

Cher's cosmetic surgeries have been well publicized over the years. In fact, she's often referred to herself as "the plastic surgery poster girl." However, Cher flatly denies reports that there are few original parts left on her beautiful frame, and says that it's absolutely untrue that she's had cheek implants and a rib removed.

"It's so stupid," Cher informed a London newspaper in 1998. "I've had my cheekbones since I was small. And it is impossible to have a rib removed! That always seemed particularly silly to me—but I will have to defend myself for the rest of my life against it."

However, Cher does 'fess up to enjoying a few benefits of cosmetic surgery, including having her breasts lifted after daughter Chastity was born. "They got so huge after the birth," she says.

Her first experience under the knife was to make her nose smaller. This decision came about when Cher saw herself on the big screen for the first time. "I looked at myself up there and thought, 'Oh, God, I'm all nose.'"

Cher has grown tired of media hounds assuming that she continues to have work done. "It bothers me sometimes, but not enough to hold back my progress."

The New Millennium

In the new millennium, fans want to know how Cher managed to "turn back time," for she seems to look younger than ever. She appears to have no wrinkles, and she is athletically fit as opposed to being simply skinny. Our favorite diva has a mature confidence that seems to reflect in her clothing, and she has recently been spotted wearing smart, black, silk pantsuits and other low-key outfits from top designers, including Rebecca Taylor and Pamela Dennis. Fluctuating between quiet elegance with a modern flair and straight-out funky-chic looks seems to suit her. It's been rumored that she's even been getting her tattoos removed by laser surgery. Cher has stated that she has outgrown them.

These days, if you'd like to purchase some of Cher's cast-offs, you can do so on eBay by bidding on items from noted seller Cherwares, who personally gets clothes from Cher's assistants. Many are Cher tops, which she wore with interesting camisoles and bodysuits underneath. Cher actually still wears some of the jewelry and scarves from her now-defunct Sanctuary collection. Cherwares also

auctions off Cher's home furnishings as she has recently remodeled her fabulous Malibu home.

Cher's personal items also started popping up for fans to purchase at Cahuenga Sid's Hollywood Bungalow at Disney World's MGM theme park. And at still another memorabilia store at Downtown Disney, some of Cher's wire-framed sunglasses and green, platform mules were going for two-hundred dollars each in 1999. Even some of her higher-end lingerie (bras and nightgowns) from top Saks Fifth Avenue designers like Fernando Sanchez popped up in these Disney World stores, as well as a few costume castoffs from *Mask*.

Makeupwise, Cher seems to be sticking with medium-to-dark lipcolors and dramatic (but not overwhelming) eye make-up, occasionally accented with colored contact lenses and false, individual lashes. She seems to complement the occasional odd-colored wig with contrasting shadows. "I could have bought five homes with what I've spent on makeup," Cher confessed in 1999. "I love going to the makeup department. People always look at your face first, so it's important to keep it looking as good as you can."

RICKY MARTIN ››
Crazy, Sexy, Drool

Entertainment
WEEKLY
#482 • April 23, 19..

Cher
An Interview
You Just Won't
'BELIEVE'

DOES Hollywood Hate Val Kilmer?

#329 • MAY 31, 1998

Entertainment
WEEKLY

CHER

CANNES
GOODS!

$2.50 (CAN. $3.50)

TV GUIDE

AUGUST 21–27 $1.79

INSIDE:
POP
SENSATION
CHRISTINA
AGUILERA
BEHIND
THE SCENES
AT BEHIND
THE MUSIC

cher

THE TRUTH ABOUT HER LOW MOMENTS, HER LONGING F...
ROMANCE AND HER LIFE'S DREAM—TO BE A GRANDMOTH...

LADIES' HOME
JOURI...

SPECIAL WOMEN'S
HEALTH SECTION

NEW CURES FOR CANCER

ALTERNATIVE MEDICINE
What Harms, What Heals

A Woman's Most
Embarrassing Ailment

SIZE 14 OR OVER?
DRESS THIN,
LOOK GREAT

**MOST REQUESTED
THANKSGIVING RECIPES**

HOW TO GET OUT OF DEBT
Step-By-Step

**SUPERMODEL BEAUTY
TRICKS EVERYONE CAN USE**

PLANE CRASH: "How I Survived"

I Love Lucy
HER OWN LOVE STORY

She's Been
Scorned,
Lovelorn,
And Laughed
At—Why
It's Finally
Fun To Be
CHER
Again

**GWYNETH
PALTROW**
ENTERS THE
TIME CAPSULE!

DO YOU KNOW
WHEN YOUR CHILD
IS TELLING A LIE?

$2.49

0 92567 14150

...C STARS WITH REAL STY...
MAY

...ebrity
style

THE
MUSIC ISSUE
WHO MATTE...
AND WHY

INSIDE:
SHANIA TWAIN
MADONNA
MICK JAGGER
TINA TURNER
SARAH McLACHLA...
JANET JACKSO...
LENNY KRAVIT...
STEVIE NICKS

Can You
'Believe' She's
Back?

CHER

Display
May ...
$3.99 US

CHAPTER SEVEN

The Nineties: Turning Back Time

Cher's big-screen experience helped her do some of the most memorable music videos, including "If I Could Turn Back Time," "Just Like Jesse James," "Love and Understanding," "Believe," and "Strong Enough."

As the eighties neared the end, Cher was in demand, but it would be a while before she'd star in another major film. She discovered that she had the "new yuppie disease" known as Epstein-Barr Syndrome.

Another thing that kept her from working in movies again for a while was the 1990 infomercial she did for friend Lori Davis's hair products. Cher had always used the Davis line and thought it would be an easy way to make money while she wasn't making films. Her manager was against the idea from the beginning. He told Cher straight out not to do it because it would ruin her credibility, not just as an actress, but as an Oscar-winning actress.

Unbeknownst to Cher, the infamous infomercial

Cher on stage: Heart of Stone Tour 1990.

was shown night and day on hundreds of cable networks across the country. (She originally thought it would air just a few times and that would be the end of it). Even David Letterman and *Saturday Night Live* began doing parodies of Cher, which probably made the backlash seem even worse. Sure, Cher's credibility was challenged, but in the nineties the invincible Cher proved she could still be as popular as ever—both as a pop-music diva and as a movie star who could keep the income rolling in.

Cher switched gears temporarily and appeared in a series of exercise videos and coauthored a health and exercise book with Dr. Richard Haas. At this point, because of her illness, Cher was concerned about her health and started working out and eating right. She also launched a hot new perfume called Uninhibited, which is now discontinued, but has been known to fetch between sixty to two hundred dollars a bottle (depending on the size).

I have five images of Cher in the 1990s. First there is Cher the rock 'n' roll high priestess she became with songs like "If I Could Turn Back Time." Secondly, there is the curiously altered post-plastic-surgery Cher of the film *Faithful*. Third, there is the Cher we saw at Sonny Bono's funeral. Fourth, there is the chic, fashionable, and classic looking Cher of the movie *Tea With Mussolini*. The character she played in this film signals a side of Cher we might again see recurring in her future films. And, finally, there is Cher—the comeback queen of her "Believe" video, and the hugely successful concert tour that hit inspired.

—Mark Bego, author of *Cher: If You Believe*

These new accomplishments gave Cher the courage to direct the first segment of *If These Walls Could Talk*. (She also starred in the segment and helped with the dialogue changes and editing for this much heralded 1993 special.) This, too, proved to be one of the highlights of her ever-expanding career. As Cher remarked, "The first day I walked onto the set, I was pretty petrified, but I thought, Well, I'm here, I might as well just do it. And soon I was thinking, This is so much fun! It was definitely a lot of work, and it really tested my stamina. But I loved it from the beginning."

On a more personal note, Cher's daughter Chastity came out about her sexuality, much to her mom's chagrin. Even though the diva had worked with and had friendships with many gays, when her darling daughter admitted she had a gal-pal, Cher allegedly went ballistic and couldn't face Chastity for a couple of weeks. Adding to her pain was that the tabloids relished the story. For nearly a month and a half, headlines from *The Star* to *The Enquirer* to *The Globe* and back again screamed the news. Cher eventually made peace

Love Hurts Tour 1992.

with Chastity and is now very accepting of any girlfriend she wants to bring over to Mom's posh Malibu house.

Mid-decade, the Dark Lady decided she wanted to go into the mail-order catalog business and imported fabulous items (most of a goth nature) to sell in her Sanctuary catalog. The venture was not a success. She had problems with the culmination of orders from the catalog's original fulfillment center in the South and found the

Cher meets the press as she premieres her new fragrance, Uninhibited, in New York City.

business to be extremely challenging on the whole. "It is more than a catalog to me," she said at the time. "I worked so hard on this creation. I personally selected all the products, some being replicas of things in my homes in Malibu and London." It was not long-lived. Some of the surplus items frequently appear on her website and certainly plenty are available on eBay for auction.

Aside from Cher's many international hit singles, she has acquired quite a strong following in Britain. In fact, she recorded her last two albums *Believe* and *Living Proof* in London.

Cher's Top Ten 1990s Singles in the United Kingdom

"Just Like Jesse James" (1990)

"The Shoop Shoop Song" (1991)

"Love Hurts" (1991)

"Love and Understanding" (1991)

"Oh, No Not My Baby" (1992)

"Could've Been You" (1992)

"Walking in Memphis" (1995)

"One by One" (1996)

"The Sun Ain't Gonna Shine Anymore" (1996)

"Believe" (1998)

"Strong Enough" (1999)

The nineties were a good time for Cher not only musically—"Believe" turned out to be the highest-charting single of her career—but the 1999 film *Tea With Mussolini* proved to be a heck of a way to end a decade. In the film, Cher played a well-heeled society matron who collects art and is duped by a much younger, charming, European cad. Cher was honored to be in the company of great actresses like Judi Dench and Maggie Smith. It was important to her to be respected by such world-class actresses after being chided for taking on the lightweight role of quirky Mrs. Flax in the 1990 comedy, *Mermaids*.

While Cher ended the decade with a couple of hit records, she also had to live through her most poignant on-camera moment of her life—

Cher Sells Seashells . . . and Other Things—
Sanctuary

The Sanctuary catalog is missed and issues have become hot collector's items. It was truly the best way for diehard fans to buy a piece of Cher's lifestyle and unique decorating tastes for themselves. Cher premiered her Sanctuary catalog, which she refers to as a coffee-table book to order from, in 1994. Sadly, it did not make it to the new millennium, though many of the items are now up for sale on both eBay and on the official Cher website, www.cher.com.

Fans loved the catalog because it not only featured commentary by Cher and the various unique items available for purchase, but because most of the items were hand selected by the Dark Lady in her travels around the globe. Mainly described by fans and critics as "heavily goth," the catalog featured a lot of wrought-iron items that were truly interesting and usually had a spiritual inspiration. A typical item would be a gargoyle objet d'art or heavy door knocker. More expensive items included coffee tables and other small pieces of furniture that fetched upward of a thousand dollars and were costly to ship. Lesser-priced items included exotic seashells, candles, candle snuffers, small glasses, and teapots. On the fashion front, there were plenty of heart- and cross-shaped pins and necklaces.

Basically, the catalog made Cher the goth Martha Stewart, although she obviously never got her own "home how-to" show. "I love a beautiful and tranquil home, it has been a necessity for me in my life," Cher wrote in one Sanctuary catalog. "My job affords me little privacy, so my home has always been my sanctuary." In each issue special symbols appeared in the item's description, letting the buyer distinguish between "a Cher favorite" or "a Cher design from her home or closet."

Many say that the demise of Sanctuary came about due to complaints of high prices. Many beg to differ, however, that believing the prices were very reasonable given the high quality of the goods.

Cher was quoted in the press when the catalog first started. Her overview of the project was that "I am a big collector of unusual objects from all over the world, mainly things that have religious symbolism or that make me feel spiritually moved. I am someone who does not have a lot of free time, obviously, but I like to comb through the great markets of the world from the Portobello Market in London to the famous weekend markets in Paris. Old things just are of better quality and obviously, of more interesting history. So if I can produce them on a high-quality level and sell them to people for a reasonable price, I feel I'm bringing them something special. This is not your run-of-the-mill commercial stuff; it has a bit of attitude and history. Also, I want to sell things that become family heirlooms . . . things that are quirky and fun but of good quality and are worth passing down."

There were various "good luck" items made from jade and other natural elements, which are supposed to bring success, health, and happiness to anyone who touches them. It would be nice to know if any of these "lucky charms" from Sanctuary actually helped out Cher fans in everyday life.

The word "sanctuary" means safe haven, and Cher was obviously trying to create the booklike catalog as an escape from dreary, everyday life for its readers. The descriptions for each item were so compelling that fans read them as if they were passages of the latest Stephen King novel.

giving a speech at Sonny Bono's memorial service. (Bono was killed an Aspen skiing accident in January 1998.) Cher claims she did not know she was being videotaped, but grieving fans appreciated the fact that the eulogy was filmed and aired on most news programs on the same night of the service. Four decades of admirers were able to hear Cher convey sweet tales of what made Sonny such a great "character" in her life, and the speech showed off her inner sensitivity and wit. Later that sad day, Cher's mom, Georgia Holt, told a reporter: "Cher told me she had to lock her knees to get through it and that she had never cried so hard in her life."

At the time of Sonny's death, the two were supposedly in negotiations for a Broadway play about their life together. Now, we'll never know what will become of that—unless Cher or Sonny's widow, Mary, tries to revive the project. It may end up as a hot Hollywood movie property some time in the next five years, like the made-for-televison film *The Beat Goes On*.

As Cher said a final good-bye to Sonny at his wake, her own life was just getting better with the release of *Believe*, which was followed by a world concert tour. The new millennium brought her an HBO *Live from Las Vegas* special, which gave tens of millions of viewers a glimpse of Cher in full regalia.

"Even in death, I don't feel separated from him," Cher has said of her first husband, Sonny Bono.

Cher sings the National Anthem in 1999.

64

JANUARY 19, 1998

People weekly

1935-1998
SONNY BONO
His improbable life
and sudden death

Sonny and then-wife
Cher in 1971

CHAPTER EIGHT

The Top Ten Cher Myths: Truth or Hype?

Since Cher began her life-in-the-public-eye, she has been viewed under a magnifying glass by the press. There have been some persistent rumors about her, and most of them are only half-truths. In this chapter, we will dispel the falsehoods and tell the truth!

Myth Number One:

Sonny and Cher's divorce was bitter, and there was a lot of fighting right up until Sonny's death in 1998.

Truth:

Sonny and Cher's divorce in 1974 caused a big commotion because up until it actually happened, the American television viewing public thought they were the happiest couple on earth. The truth of the matter is that Cher instigated the divorce not only because she felt that Sonny had her under his thumb in every way, but she was freaked out to find that Sonny's lawyers had set up a company called Cher Enterprises, in which she was simply an employee who only received a small percent of the earnings. Rumor has it that episode was the final straw in the shaky marriage of Sonny and Cher. Rumors also abounded that Sonny was unfaithful, although there is no evidence of that at the time.

When Cher parted ways with Sonny, she did not even know how to write out a check because, as she puts it, "He always took care of everything." Cher felt she had grown up and wanted to be more in control of her life. During their sepa-

Sonny: The man who brought Cher fame.

ration, Sonny and Cher lived in their Bel Air home with Sonny on one end, accompanied by his girlfriend/secretary, Connie Forman, and Cher alone on the other end. By all accounts, it was a happy arrangement, although the Dark Lady now admits that it was sort of strange.

Sonny and Cher's divorce was an amicable one. They were even able to do the *Sonny & Cher Show* on television show together after their divorce. It was never as successful as the original

Cher on Sonny & Cher: "We were like Siamese twins—joined at the heart."

Sonny & Cher Comedy Hour because as one former CBS executive put it, "It seemed insincere and the real fans felt cheated."

The years immediately following the divorce showed that Sonny and Cher kept in touch with each other at least a couple of times a month, which eventually petered out to only a few times a year. When Sonny and Cher were reunited on *Late Night with David Letterman* in 1987, they sang "I Got You Babe" and held hands; it seemed like old times. Cher later admitted that she

thought Letterman put her on the spot and she wasn't happy about it at all.

In the year before Sonny's death, the former sixties duo were on the phone on a more regular basis discussing doing a Broadway play based on their rise to fame and its aftermath. By the end of 2000, rumors abounded that it was supposed to be called *The Beat Goes On* (same title of as the ABC movie-of-the-week), but this was not confirmed by any of Cher's press representatives.

Cher's touching eulogy at Sonny's January

Under the magnifying glass: Cher meets the press.

1998 wake was one of the most sincere (and most televised) in Hollywood history. Her sentiments were without a doubt, straight from the heart. Cher genuinely expressed gratitude for all the emotional and show business support her ex-husband and singing partner had given her over the years.

So, what about all the supposed post-marriage feuding? No doubt it didn't go beyond the immediate decision on Cher's part in 1974 to separate from the man that had brought her fame. It was touch and go back then, but Sonny and Cher would always be soul mates and would never really ever be out of each other's lives. Still, after Sonny's death, Cher did sue his estate for one million in back alimony when the entire estate was supposedly only worth two million. Sonny was not worth much due to the fact that he had been living on a politician's salary after he gave up his Palm Springs eatery a few years before.

Sonny and Cher are the perfect example of a couple who were open-minded enough to stay friends and to not let their divorce affect either their friendship or professional relationship. However, toward the end of his life, Sonny still

seemed shocked that Cher divorced him, because he considered Sonny and Cher "to be forever." In a way, they are still living out "forever" in the hearts and minds of their most loyal fans.

Myth Number Two:

Cher has had a tremendous amount of plastic surgery.

Truth:

Sure, Jay Leno and Conan O'Brien might make it a regular point to discuss Cher's "synthetic body parts" as part of their late-night monologues, but this rumor is something that has been discussed by fans and media alike ever since Cher's solo variety show went off the air in the late seventies.

Due to her ever-changing looks, especially around the time she started to get into serious acting around 1980, tongues started wagging about what she'd had "done." Suddenly everyone was talking about rib removal, acid-bath skin lightening, and even some freak operations that don't really exist.

In 1999 and even more recently, Cher has

Will there ever be a Broadway play based on the lives of Sonny and Cher?

admitted to having her nose fixed, two breast augmentations, ("My chest had gotten huge when I was pregnant, and my skin got stretched out real bad. So I had it tightened up. It's a fabulous procedure that really works.") and braces to straighten her teeth. She apparently did not partake in the alleged eye lift, cheek implants, tummy tucks, butt lifts, or liposuction that were a big part of the relentless hearsay.

Cher is especially angry about the rib-removal rumors that have always persisted, especially since that is a dangerous and rarely done operation. According to some New York–based plastic surgeons, the only place in the world where this procedure is common is in Brazil. (The procedure was done frequently in the States back when the Jayne Mansfield–type figure was popular in the late fifties and early sixties.)

Cher has also admitted to having her tattoos removed and collagen injections to make her lips fuller.

Cher is realistic about the significance Hollywood places on appearances, and she knows she always has to look her best in order to get many of the roles she covets. As Cher has stated: "Show me anyone who wants to be disposable or without sex appeal. There's no value in getting older, especially in show business. We're a visual society. I didn't make this society. I just live in it. I'd like to look really great for as long as I can."

Seeing herself on the big screen in *Silkwood* gave her a strong dose of reality about how big her nose was. She was also upset about the prominence of a bump on the bridge. She remarked later: "When I saw my face ten feet tall in close-ups, it's a little different from just talking to somebody on the street. I wanted my nose done because it really bothered me. My teeth were straightened and brought out with braces and a retainer. It improved the shape of my mouth. Maybe that's why people think I've had cheek and chin implants."

Cher's toned body is largely the result of working out, not lying under a physician's knife. She says, "It's my body to do with what I want. If some people think that makes me terminally vain, then yes, I am vain." In early 2002, the Dark Lady was battling rumors again bandied about by catty reporters that her "face is caving in." However, on a West Greenwich Village street filming her "Song for the Lonely" video, many who saw her would say she looked as divine as ever. Plus, she was able to keep up with the twenty-something professional dancers' hot steppin'.

Loyal followers will always attest that Cher's young look is not really due to a surgeon's knife or anything physical at all, but rather a youthful and positive attitude about life. Plus, she has always had the latest and trendiest fashions with a slew of trusted stylists who know what look she wants to achieve in dressing that body.

Myth Number Three:

Cher had a poverty-stricken childhood.

Truth:

Since the sixties, Cher has always freely admitted that she was poor a lot of the time growing up, but that there were bouts of middle-class and even upper-crust living. It all depended on whom her much-wedded, sometimes-actress mom, Georgia, was romantically involved with at the time. She admits that her mom was usually drawn to poor men (such as Cher's drifter drug-addict father, John Sarkisian), although Georgia always verbalized that she wanted a wealthy husband.

In the late fifties, when her mom was married to millionaire-builder Joseph Harper Collins (whom she met at a party at affluent socialite Doris Duke's house), Cher and her family lived what she calls "la dolce vita." Captured by her high-cheekboned beauty, Collins proposed to Cher's mom only fifteen minutes after they'd met. So Georgia and family moved from a teeny, red house on Beeman Avenue in the San Fernando Valley to an opulent mansion in Beverly Hills. Cher not only loved her surroundings, but adored her big, stocky stepfather, who she thought was fun to be around.

Cher recalled her entry into Beverly Hills society and how it simply "blew her mind." Everything was changed for the young, teenage girl. Now she was taking a school bus with Tina Sinatra, whom she thought was so beautiful, and she ate real steak for the first time. Lobster became her favorite food, and she always had her friends over to the house for parties and barbecues.

Sadly for Cher and her sister, Georgeanne, the party was over when the Collins's marriage ended after only five short months. Cher's family then moved to the Valley for a while and then finally wound up back in the dreaded little red house on Beeman Avenue.

Later on, in the early sixties, Cher tasted middle-class urban life in New York City when her mom was married to Gilbert LaPierre, whose surname Cher took as a teen. They lived in a two-bedroom, doorman, elevator building that would probably cost five grand a month these days—but only cost one hundred or so dollars back then. Cher was impressed by Manhattan and what it had to offer, but at the same time was afraid to venture out on her own. She hung out with the beatnik set a little, and this is probably where her eccentric taste in clothing came from.

That Cher grew up poverty-stricken is partially true. But Cher probably experienced being in every socioeconomic group as she was growing up, thanks to the several different men her mom had married. Cher admits that her odd childhood was echoed in her film *Mermaids*, and that she based her character on her moody, eccentric, but caring mom, Georgia.

Myth Number Four:

Cher is a hopeless shopaholic.

Truth:

There is no question that Cher loves to shop. She's even been known to go on shopping sprees while doing interviews, which the New York *Daily News* music writer Jim Farber can attest to. While writing a piece about her *Living Proof* CD, Cher and Farber managed to spend an hour in the Otto Tootsi Plohound shoe store on East Fifty-seventh Street and still get in a serious heart-to-heart chat about both her personal and professional lives.

Cher has a warehouse full of her more collectable clothes, and it consists of 80 percent Bob

Mackie creations. Yes, she saved all those fabulous gowns from the old *Sonny & Cher Comedy Hour* days, although she cannot fit into them due to having a more muscular, toned body these days. Cher does recognize their importance in fashion history, and recently lent them to an FIT (Fashion Institute of Technology) exhibit of the "Best of Bob Mackie." Everything was there, from the famous Laverne outfit to the "Gypsies, Tramps and Thieves" Native American, white suede, sequined number with its revealing side slits.

Believe it or not, during a concert tour or movie shoot, Cher very often does not go shopping for three months at a time. However, when she does shop, she is one of those "give me one in every color" people, and often items never get worn simply because she buys so much. Cher's shopping excesses goes to several places. She donates items to various charities so that they can be auctioned off at fund-raising events, including those for her pet charity, the Children's Craniofacial Foundation. In the mid- to late-eighties, hundreds wound up for sale at good prices at Susie's Coelho's A Star Is Worn boutique. Cher's willingness to give hundreds of items to Sonny's then-wife's Susie, store shows just how close she was to Sonny and how there were really no hard feelings after the divorce.

These days, you can buy Cher's like-new castoffs at Hollywood memorabilia stores like Sid Cahuenga's Hollywood Bungalow at the MGM theme park at Disney World. More shoes than anything else pop up in these stores, since Cher is rumored to have hundreds in her spacious walk-in closets and storage facilities at any given time. Judging from the condition they are in, she probably wears them once or twice and then gives them away.

Myth Number Five:

Cher moved from one home to another in her youth and it gave her the insecure feeling of having "no roots."

Truth:

For Cher, it was her looks, and not all the moving around, that gave her her basic insecurity. Cher readily admits that she would rather be an all-American beauty and often cites actress and friend Michelle Pfeiffer as the woman whose looks she'd give her right arm for.

Cher was always the dark one in her family—meaning dark hair, dark eyes, and dark skin. It wasn't just that blondes were the pretty ones. According to Cher, blondes were also the "good" ones; women with black hair like hers were either evil queens or witches in many kids' movies.

In 1961, *Breakfast at Tiffany's* came out, and Cher was happy to see the leading character was offbeat looking. So she emulated her in every way, right down to the giant leave-me-alone black sunglasses. After that, Cher realized that maybe being different wasn't so bad after all.

Cher also acknowledges that moving around so much meant she had to switch schools a lot of the time. But Cher had a good attitude about making new friends and didn't judge people on looks and how much money they had. Going to racially mixed schools in different neighborhoods in the Los Angeles area also made her "color blind," something she is grateful for to this day.

So in actuality, Cher is someone who typifies the fact that you can live a vagabond childhood and still have your head on straight. Her early life also made Cher willing to date different kinds of guys, both when she was growing up and later in her adult years. Her mother's adventurous attitude toward everyday life most likely helped Cher to become the strong-minded woman she is today.

On a sentimental note, Cher has always admired her mom, who gave Cher and her sister, Georgeanne, plenty of love and support and always put them first. "My mom was one of the first-ever spontaneous people, and she was very much like my early idol, Holly Golightly." Cher has said. "I would have to say that whatever is written about my mom, I couldn't have asked for anyone more loving and caring."

Myth Number Six:

Cher only dates "boy toys."

Truth:

This is truly an unfair accusation that stemmed from the fact that tabloids referred to Rob Camilletti not only as "Cher's bagel boy," but simply as her "boy toy" as well.

Certainly Cher has had her share of much younger men, including Tom Cruise and Val Kilmer, who are both about twenty years younger than she is, but for the most part, she has dated men who are in their thirties through fifties and would hardly qualify as boy toys. Good examples of this would be Gene Simmons and David Geffen. So the real truth is that Cher's had more "men toys" than "boy toys."

And the tabloid term "boy toy" should not be used so loosely, since Cher did have a long-term, live-in relationship with Camilletti. As Cher told a reporter a few years ago, "They called him my boy toy, but he is one of the most mature guys I have ever met."

Because of all the boy toy accusations by the press, Cher has kept her recent liaisons private, although she claims to have recently taken a four-year break from dating. Nothing has leaked out from Cher's private circle except for the fact that Camilletti lives at her house from time to time, usually when she's on the road or out of the country.

Cher says that she'll probably never marry again, and that wouldn't be surprising. She's had an exciting enough love life thus far, and she's had enough drama for ten divine divas. The question most asked by fans these days is will Cher ever find lasting love?

Myth Number Seven:

Cher has the Epstein-Barr virus, which is really just an imaginary disease.

Truth:

Cher was diagnosed with Epstein-Barr in the late eighties and reportedly had to cancel shows due to the exhaustion it caused. While many people think this New Age disease is "fake," it certainly has taken it's toll on Cher. As a result, she does not do lengthy tours anymore and has a personal physician on call who has done groundbreaking research on this mysterious illness.

Cher actually began to suffer the first symptoms of the debilitating illness on the *Witches of Eastwick* set, and that's when it got reported in daily newspapers and *Time* and *People* magazines. "It started off as chronic fatigue syndrome when I was making *Witches of Eastwick*," Cher recalled in an interview years later. "It's a strange disease. No one knows enough about it yet. You have to learn to recognize your symptoms and let your body rest. I have just learned to take it easy, eat properly, and not push my body too far when it happens; rest is the most important thing."

The Epstein-Barr virus is thought to be responsible for a number of diseases in addition to glandular fever (otherwise known as infectious mononucleosis) and Burkitt's lymphoma. One of these is nasopharyngeal carcinoma: this is a tumor of the nasal passages and throat, which affects up to 2 percent of the people in southern China and also occurs in Southeast Asia, northern Africa, and among Arctic peoples. It has been proposed as a possible cause of Hodgkin's disease (a type of cancer affecting cells of lymph nodes).

People infected with the Epstein-Barr virus will retain it for life, but it may not make them sick. In fact, the virus infects almost everyone in developing countries and more than 80 percent of people in developed countries. It is spread mainly via the transfer of saliva between individuals,

which is the reason that glandular fever has been dubbed the "kissing disease." (Of course, that doesn't mean Cher got it from kissing).

Myth Number Eight:

Cher has dyslexia.

Truth:

This is completely true, although it has never been reported just how significant her dyslexia really is. People who have spent time with Cher know she has to have all her friends and family on speed dial because she can't dial the digits in the correct order.

Fortunately for Cher, her dyslexia has not caused that much of a problem in everyday affairs since she obviously does not have to type or write for a living. She was supposedly a bit embarrassed about it at first, but then realized there are tens of millions of other Americans dealing with the same disability.

Myth Number Nine:

Cher suffers hopelessly from stage fright.

Truth:

As far as every report goes, this is entirely true—especially when it comes to singing in front of a live audience. As a matter of fact, Sonny & Cher was really just supposed to be *Cher*; Sonny only joined Cher onstage because she was too petrified to go out there alone! She was even too shy to sing by herself back in the days when Sonny worked at producer Phil Spector's Hollywood studio, and it took a lot of coaxing by her future husband for her to take the mike alone.

Cher has admitted to having to cross her knees so she doesn't fall down during her severe bouts of stage fright. She confesses that some of her worst bouts in recent years were delivering Sonny's eulogy and singing the National Anthem at the 1997 Superbowl. She also came under a lot of criticism for recording her vocal, ahead of

time, but she did it to ensure perfection once she got out on the gridiron.

Cher stresses that some of her biggest episodes of nervousness were not necessarily when she had the biggest audiences to face. She states, "I hated playing Vegas when we were on

our comeback or whatever you call it. I think I really hated doing those lounge songs and felt like I wasn't being true to myself. But we had to do those shows or else we'd starve. I dreaded going out there and seeing those smarmy businessmen in their leisure suits. It was like every performer's worst nightmare."

These days, Cher says she still gets a little nervous to go out before a crowd, mainly because her live show has so many sets and style changes. Cher, ever the perfectionist, worries that something will go wrong. "I have a great staff," she said. "It takes hundreds of people to work on my show and keep it flowing right. I worry that a light will fall or that I will fall flat on my face. I also worry that I won't have the energy to complete a show. People say I am tough on myself, but the bigness of it all overwhelms me and I still have insecurities about my talents. I'm just Cher and I have my rough spots."

In a way, it's comforting to think that such a legendary superstar like Cher still has her insecurities. But honestly, as thousands would agree, when has Cher ever performed a clunker of a show? Each concert in the past twenty years has proved to be a musical spectacular, and Cher's off-the-cuff remarks to the audience are always clever and humorous.

Myth Number Ten:

Cher has a fascination with both goth and biker lifestyles.

Truth:

This is fairly true, but Cher has many fascinations with many types of lifestyles. She is anything but the typical, boring, rich, Beverly Hills celebrity driving around town in a white Rolls and heading to Rodeo Drive to shop for the new Gucci bag that everyone else in town is carrying. Cher projects a true respect for lifestyles beyond her immediate, luxurious environment. While she has had her share of scandalous goth- and biker-style getups, these looks have certainly been assimilated into the American mainstream culture in the past fifteen years. And Cher has helped the American public accept what was normally thought of as a "tough" look for a woman.

As for goth, that fascination probably originated with her love for the mystical in general and the fact that so many musicians started sporting that all-black look back in the early days of heavy metal. And remember, she dated guys with a pseudo-goth look back in the late seventies and through late eighties—like Gene Simmons and

Richie Sambora. Cher's long, black locks were always naturally "goth looking," even way back in the sixties when she first became famous.

Fans are fascinated that Cher seems to be the only over-fifty star pulling off the biker and goth look (not including Billy Bob Thornton or Ozzy Osbourne). Cher's youthful attitude seems to let her pull off dressing in these styles when most women her age would be laughed out of town.

Rumor has it that Cher's interest in biker culture started when she was married to Gregg Allman, also a Harley lover. Gregg rode around Hollywood with Cher accompanying him and they were quite the eye-catching couple. Later, when she was dating Les Dudek—lead guitarist of her early eighties group Black Rose and ace session player—they were seen together on their hogs as well. Cher also rides her own Harley in a few charity races each year.

"Biker culture" is such a part of the mainstream these days that no one would think twice about a celebrity being into it, but twenty-seven years ago, when Cher first got into riding Harleys, it raised a few eyebrows, especially for a female celebrity known best for her glitzy gowns. Later on, Cher shared her love of bikes with Richie Sambora and Val Kilmer.

" . . . I still have insecurities about my talents. I'm just Cher and I have my rough spots."

CHAPTER NINE

Do You Believe in Love? The Men in Cher's Life

Men are luxuries, not necessities. I don't need a man, but I'm happier with one.—Cher

Cher's love life has been as colorful as her songs and attire—but everyone already knows that. In the early days, she preferred older men; more recently it's been younger men. Cher is generally unpredictable in everything she does, but with men, she clearly went from powerful men that could help her career to young, fun, hip guys that she dated purely because she was attracted to them. While some of the men on this list never publicly acknowledged that they've dated the Dark Lady, enough music-business insiders have remarked that she has been linked to them.

Cher is often spotted out on the town, holding hands with one of her amours (even if she has denied dating them). Cher vows she will never marry again, but she also says she will never stop believing in love. "A girl can wait for the right man to come along," she explained in one 1980 interview, "but in the meantime that still doesn't mean she can't have a wonderful time with all the wrong ones."

Cher has been connected to a variety of male admirers not mentioned in this list, including actor Matt Damon, musician Mark Lennon, *Goodfellas* star Ray Liotta, Broadway leading man John Barrowman, and young *Tea with Mussolini* costar Paolo Seganti. Many have asked Cher why she doesn't seem to be attracted to older men since the days of Sonny. Or does it just appear that way? "If I waited for men my own age to ask me out," she has said, "I would never have a date."

"There's something about older men. They just don't like me for some reason. I'm happier with younger men. They are definitely more fun!"

Here's a look at some of those fun guys to whom Cher has been linked.

Warren Beatty

Actor/director. Dated late 1962.

Warren Beatty was one of Hollywood's most famous ladies' men when he met Cher. She was only sixteen at the time, and they dated a couple of months. They literally met on the streets of Hollywood, and soon, the young Cher was showing up at Beatty's Hollywood Hills bachelor pads (they really didn't go out on dates).

Once Beatty called Cher's house and asked her mother, Georgia, to put her on the phone. Georgia alluded to Cher's age and, as Cher claims in her book *The First Time*, it actually made him like her better.

Cher was never clear about why the relationship ended, but most likely the then-twenty-something Beatty came to his senses about dating a minor and stopped calling. Undoubtedly, the legendary Romeo was juggling at least a dozen starlets and Sunset Strip types at the time.

The ultra-private Beatty, who has said that he'd rather ride naked on a camel through the desert then give an interview, has never made a public statement about his relationship with Cher.

• •

Sonny Bono

Singer/songwriter/record producer/television star/politician. (1964–1975. Lived with Cher 1964–1969; married her in 1969; divorced in 1975.

Sonny is covered in other areas of this book, but one can't say enough about the man who had enough faith in then–Hollywood-wannabe-Cher to fully support her talents and get her introduced to the right people.

Cher has admitted over the years that she was initially attracted to the then-twenty-eight-year-old, newly separated Sonny because not only was he a record producer, but he promised he could help catapult her to fame. So it was a relationship based on opportunity as much as love. Of course, audiences who came to know them as the fur-vested sixties hippie couple holding hands and singing "I Got You Babe," and the ultimate seventies funny and ultra-hip television couple, believed the relationship was purely starry-eyed.

Sadly, their relationship started to unravel while still doing the *Sonny & Cher Comedy Hour*. Cher thought Sonny was too much of a control freak for her to handle anymore. Though divorced, they remained friends until Sonny's death.

Sonny spent his later years as a restaurateur, the mayor of Palm Springs, and as a United States congressman. His untimely demise left both his family and fans shocked and saddened.

• •

Bill Hamm

Guitar player with the Sonny & Cher band. Dated 1972–1973.

It comes as a shock to Sonny & Cher fans, but the marriage was unraveling long before their divorce. And, as noted in the television movie about the famous couple, Cher often had post-show, hotel-room liaisons with the couple's guitar player, Bill Hamm. The tall, cool, good-looking axeman supposedly felt guilty about "getting it on" with the boss's wife, but Sonny could not do much, as he had been unfaithful long before then.

Sonny and Cher's marriage ended, but their love is, without a doubt, eternal.

David Paich

Conductor/keyboard player with Sonny & Cher (later keyboardist/songwriter for seventies rock band Toto). Dated 1972–1973.

David Paich was the chiseled-looking keyboard player who was Cher's second post-Sonny boyfriend. He went on to play on some of the seventies' biggest records as the keyboardist and primary songwriter of Toto. Cher has never spoken much about him, except that he made her laugh on the road when she was tired of doing Las Vegas performances, the least favorite aspect of her career.

Bernie Taupin

Songwriting partner to Elton John. Dated 1973.

This is one of those relationships that no one close to Cher can either confirm or deny. The quiet, charming, sensitive, former Englishman (now an American citizen) responsible for all the great lyrics to Elton John's songs has never admitted to dating Cher. The rumors were started when Cher and Bernie were caught dining around Hollywood around the time Cher was thinking of starting work on a new album. Most likely, the lyricist was thinking of penning material for a Cher album, and then got too busy writing for a new Elton record. In other words, there's a strong possibility that their relationship was purely platonic. However, Bernie Taupin did end up writing a song for Cher years later when she was in her hard rock band Black Rose in 1980. The song was titled "Julie."

David Geffen

Record/movie producer. Dated 1973–1974.

Known as one of Hollywood's hottest players, Cher met David Geffen when she signed with his label back in 1973. The self-admitted bisexual businessman attracted Cher not only because he was a "serious" member of the Hollywood community who believed in her talents, but because he offered her full creative control in the studio. He even allowed her to put together her own group, Black Rose, with whom she both toured and recorded in the early and mid-seventies. Cher has admitted that she was impressed with the distinguished-looking Geffen because of his infinite wisdom. She has also remarked that he is "the smartest man I've ever met."

Alan Gorrie

Keyboardist of Average White Band. Dated 1975.

Alan Gorrie was the guy Cher was dating the week she met Gregg Allman during one of his shows at the famed Los Angeles nightspot the Troubadour. Interestingly enough, Alan overdosed at the same party for Gregg Allman at which bandmate Robbie McIntosh overdosed. A smart, on-her-toes Cher kept her beau up and walking around after an accidental dose of strychnine-laced heroin. Sadly, McIntosh did not survive.

Greg Allman

Rock star, the Allman Brothers and occasional actor. Dated 1975; married 1975–78.

Her two husbands, Sonny Bono and Gregg Allman, couldn't have been more different. Cher's second husband, Gregg Allman, was by most accounts an irresponsible rock star and drug addict when he married Cher in Las Vegas in 1975 after a whirlwind romance. He abandoned Cher on their honeymoon; she filed for divorce nine days later, but then changed her mind. Gregg and Cher's on-again, off-again rocky relationship was all over the tabloids. The couple's divorce was finalized three years after the marriage's shaky beginning.

In the past, Cher often talked about Gregg's tenderness, but also the fact that he was only around about six months of their entire union. He seemed to either be on the road or scoring drugs. "I was so naïve about drugs then," she has said. "We were a disaster waiting to happen. There was something about Gregory. He was so handsome and so wild. He was also tender and sensitive, too."

Today, Greg Allman is clean and sober and remarried with children. He still tours with the Allman Brothers as well as performing solo shows.

Gene Simmons

Kiss's bass player. Dated 1978–1980.

Cher fans were shocked when their idol took on her first heavy metal man—one with a ten-inch tongue, to boot. The story goes that the dynamic duo met at a Hollywood party and became inseparable afterward. The relationship didn't last long.

Some say that the relationship was based on photo ops, not on love, although Cher and Simmons truly matched wits and enjoyed each other's company. It's common knowledge that Simmons has never been a one-woman man and most likely, Cher got tired of his playing around.

Cher has said despite Simmons's rough, rock-star image, he was really "rather soft" on the inside and she didn't want to get married because she realized that it wasn't true love. After Cher, Gene Simmons moved on to one of her close friends at the time, Diana Ross.

In spite of everything, over the years, the ever-sentimental Cher still has a soft spot for her old flame, and he for her. She was reunited with him in 1998 following her triumphant performance on the American Music Awards. Simmons was waiting backstage after Cher had belted out her number-one hit of the year, "Believe." He gave her a a big congratulatory hug and kiss.

Les Dudek

Rock guitarist of the late seventies hard rock band Black Rose. Dated 1980–1982.

Cher and Les worked together in Black Rose. He was the lead singer. The handsome, long-haired biker type was a quiet guy who never really spoke about his relationship with the noted diva. Cher supposedly was attracted to him one day when they met in a recording studio because he was unassuming and seemed like a "man's man." However, their personal or musical union didn't last long. The self-titled *Black Rose* album bombed. Dudek decided to pursue a solo career, while Cher packed her bags and headed for New York to reinvent herself as an actress.

Ron Duguay

New York Rangers hockey player. Dated 1982.

Cher dated this hockey legend for a couple of months after catching one of his games. Chastity has always said that the twenty-four-year-old Duguay was one of her mom's favorite boyfriends—that his sunny disposition always kept her laughing and that he was anything but a "dumb jock." After his romance (or during as some say) with Cher, it was reported that the hockey legend dated Broadway star Patti Lupone.

John Heard

Actor. Dated 1982.

This award-winning actor is the strong, silent type who prefers to stay out of the Hollywood spotlight. Not a lot is known about their relationship except that Cher heeded his advice about acting. He supposedly got her interested in more serious roles. Heard, as has been reported, was on the rebound from a short marriage to *Superman* movie actress, Margot Kidder.

Cher with Eric Stoltz, circa 1984.

John Loffler

Singer. Dated 1982–1983.

Little is known about this then-aspiring rock singer-songwriter and session man who met Cher at a music-business party in 1982. Apparently he was about to sign a recording contract the same year, but it never happened.

Val Kilmer

Actor, 1982–1984.

This famed and "chiseled" actor who has done everything from Shakespearean plays to portraying Jim Morrison in *The Doors* movie was spotted on Cher's arm when he was just a fledging thes-

pian. Fifteen years her junior, gossips' tongues were a-waggin' when Cher and Kilmer first started appearing together at Hollywood parties. Cher has always said that she liked the young actor's down-to-earth qualities, which included writing love poems, his interest in Native-American rights issues, and wanting to avoid being seen as a "star" by the press.

Eric Stoltz

Actor. Dated 1984.

Many fans were aghast when Cher began dating *Mask* costar Eric Stoltz because he played her teenaged son, Rocky, in the movie. Though Cher and Stoltz tried to keep their relationship low-key, the ever ferocious paparazzi around Hollywood "outed" them with their constant shutter bugging. Cher has always said they were just close friends and that she liked his "infinite wisdom for such a young guy," but too many industry insiders said that they were seen together a little too much to be "just friends."

Josh Donen

Television executive. Dated 1984–1986.

Josh Donen was a television executive whom Cher met during a meeting at a major network. They hit it off. Cher has said she loved his spirit of adventure and how he seemed like such a "nonexecutive type for an executive." Donen seemed to bask in the limelight of being photographed with one of the most famous women in the world on a regular basis, but supposedly, out of the limelight, he was very protective of his significant other and gave her good career advice. Cher may have encouraged Donen to get a tattoo, but he couldn't sway her into marriage. Cher turned down his proposal, but she confessed to wanting to have his baby. Because Donen was a television executive, fans had hoped he would be

What Cher found appealing about Josh Donen was his spirit of adventure and how he seemed, she stated, "a nonexecutive type for an executive."

able to convince Cher to take on a network show again. Of course, he never did.

Tom Cruise

Actor. Dated 1985–1986.

Tom Cruise was twenty-three and on the fringe of becoming a major movie star when he dated Cher. In fact, they both did their best to keep their relationship under wraps since it would be ideal fodder for the tabloids. However, Cher and Cruise still made the tabloids, much to their chagrin. Supposedly, the two met at the premiere of *Risky Business*, but didn't hook up until years later. They dated for several months and again, Cher was not ready to be married again. Cruise later wed actress Mimi Rogers, then thirty-three. Over the years, Cruise has never publicly admitted to a relationship with Cher. But of course, Hollywood insiders know different.

Rob Camilletti

Actor/bartender. Dated 1986–1989.

Rob Camilletti strolled into Twirl, a hot Tribeca nightclub one night in 1989 and time stood still for Cher. She didn't care that he was eighteen years younger and a bagel baker in Brooklyn, the dark-haired diva thought Rob was the handsomest man she had ever seen. She admired his ability to do "man's man" kind of activities, including fixing up her Greenwich Village loft.

Rob was intimidated by Cher at first, and was petrified on their first date, which was to a Broadway play premiere. Soon he learned how comfortable he could be in his older girlfriend's stardust world. It was working for Cher as well. She was finally feeling emotionally secure with a man which she hadn't felt since Sonny.

Cher has said her love with Rob Camilletti was built on simple things like holding hands, cuddling on the sofa, dining in quiet restaurants, and watching television together. "He was definitely the grown-up in our relationship. I will never stop loving him," she has said.

Cher and Rob had fun together and enjoyed each other's company. When Cher's hectic schedule allowed, the couple went to movie marathons, danced the night away in clubs, and spent quiet evenings alone. With Cher's encouragement, Camellitti took acting lessons from famed drama coach Stella Adler and eventually found small movie roles. Cher gave him his first big break portraying, what else, her main squeeze in her popular 1987 video for "I Found Someone." This led to another role in the film *Loverboy*. However, being known as Cher's boyfriend encumbered Camelletti's acting career.

Toward the end of their relationship, Cher had to bail out Camilletti, who allegedly punched a paparazzi photographer who was staking out Cher's house. The relationship supposedly ended when the temptations of Hollywood became too much and he started seeing other women. He told Cher: "I love you, but can't bear to be under this microscope all the time. I miss my life. I need to go back home."

Cher says they are still good friends today, but insiders say they are much more. Camilletti has been living in her Malibu home and bartending in Hollywood for the past two years. He appeared in her 1996 HBO movie *If These Walls Could Talk* as an abortion protester.

● ●

Richie Sambora

Bon Jovi guitarist. Dated 1989–1990.

Hard rock fans often wonder if Richie Sambora and Gene Simmons, who know each other well, ever compared notes on Cher. At forty-four, Cher went backstage at a Bon Jovi concert after the show and her eyes met Richie's across a crowded dressing room. Richie's cool, Jersey-boy style and his ability to put her at ease made Cher even more attracted to him.

Sambora, thirteen years Cher's junior, has always been known to be a charmer and was the perfect remedy for Cher to ease the heartbreak caused by Camilletti. The rock guitarist copro-

With Richie Sambora at the 1988 American Music Awards.

duced, with Jon Bon Jovi, Cher's 1987 self-titled album.

Like many of the superstar's precious beaus, Sambora was fun to be with, though at the time he was definitely not marriage material. Today, he is married to actress Heather Locklear. They are the parents of a baby girl named Eva. Richie and Cher really haven't kept in touch over the years, but have said "Hi, how are you?" in passing at awards shows, including the MTV Awards.

● ●

Eric Clapton

Rock star. Dated 1991.

Little is known about Cher's liaison with rock guitar god Eric Clapton, but it was rumored that they met through mutual musician pals in Los Angeles. Supposedly their relationship started after an all-star jam session, but it only lasted on and off for three months. Clapton has not ever spoken about his relationship with Cher to the press.

CHAPTER TEN

Cher on Film

On film, Cher started out as a sixties teen singing on the beach and made her way to worldly grand dame traveling through Europe during World War II. All sorts of future projects are in the works, but one thing's for certain: Cher's up for anything when it comes to sinking her teeth into a starring role on the big screen. Die-hard fans know that even before she met Sonny in 1964, she dreamed of making it in movies and that music was merely a detour, even though she excelled in it.

Cher's roles are few and far between, not only because it took her awhile to break into "legit" Hollywood, but because of her recording, concert, and television demands over the years. Most recently, she was hired for but then passed on the role that Sigourney Weaver took in the film *Heartbreakers*.

Now, this is the Cher filmography—big, small, and all in between! The informative listing begins with her most recent projects and runs backward, just so you can see how much Cher, the award-winning actress, has progressed in the fickle but fantastic world of moviemaking. (Film reviews are by Anne M. Raso)

(Note: *Wild on the Beach* and *Chastity* never made it to video or DVD. All other titles are available on both.)

Tea With Mussolini
(1999)

Director: Franco Zeffirelli.
Cast: Cher, Judi Dench, Maggie Smith,
Joan Plowright, and Lily Tomlin.

In this gently comic coming-of-age story, which is set in Florence, Italy, over the course of the 1930s and 1940s, the illegitimate son of an Italian merchant is raised by a group of prim, English ladies whose passion for Italian culture have made them

permanent residents. With the rise of Mussolini and the outbreak of war, the ladies are interred as prisoners, and the boy risks his life to help them. It's a lushly photographed ensemble piece that instills in the viewer Zeffirelli's contagious passion for Italian art and affection for these brave ladies. The beautiful city of Florence is at the heart of this story, based on director Franco Zeffirelli's autobiography.

It's the 1930s, and young Luca (Charlie Lucas), the illegitimate son of an Italian businessman, is taken in by a group of proper English ladies known as "Il Scorpioni" (for their "sting"). He acquires a passion for the arts as he follows them on their excursions through various museums and cathedrals, and finds his first taste of love when he falls for an extravagant Jewish American named Elsa, portrayed by Cher. When Mussolini's fascist regime joins the Nazis, the older ladies become prisoners of war, and Elsa finds herself in even greater danger. Luckily, the now-older Luca is on hand to help.

While most Cher fans felt they didn't get to see enough of their favorite idol because she had to share the spotlight with several grand dames, they did love her performance (particularly when she sang) and outrageously lavish garb, including a chinchilla-trimmed suit that would have made Bob Mackie proud!

If These Walls Could Talk
(1997)

Directors: Nancy Savoca and Cher.
Cast: Demi Moore, Sissy Spacek, Cher, Anne Heche, Jada Pinkett, Eileen Brennan, Lindsay Crouse, Joanna Gleason, CCH Pounder, and Rita Wilson.

Set in a single, suburban house, this made-for-cable trilogy examines the evolution of a woman's right to choose in three disparate years: 1952, 1974, and 1996. From the pre–Roe v. Wade back-alley option, to the mid-seventies struggle between conscience and career, to the controversy faced in the nineties, the much-discussed issue is given its due.

The first tale chronicles a woman's disheartening efforts to abort her baby during the 1950s, when the procedure was still illegal. The second story takes place in the seventies, and centers on a married mom who's just returned to college. Her attempt to balance home life and school is shattered when she discovers she's pregnant. The final tale is told from the points of view of a pro-choice pregnant woman and her pro-life roommate, and how their disagreement results in violence.

This film marks Cher's directorial debut (she directed the segment in which she appeared), and she now admits that she was "super nervous." Cher also portrays a gynecologist in the final story, which some fans snickered at, but she was indeed quite convincing. A strong proponent of women's rights, this was a real labor of love for our heroine.

Faithful
(1996)

Director: Paul Mazursky
Cast: Cher, Chazz Palminteri, Ryan O'Neal,
Elisa Leonetti (Maria); Mark Nassar, Jeffrey Wright,
David Merino, Steven Randazzo, and Olinda Turturro.

In this very dark comedy, a wife of twenty years receives an unusual gift for her anniversary—her husband has hired a hit-man to kill her. Things don't go quite as planned, though, when the hired gun and his bound target end up bonding with each other. Chazz Palminteri adapted the screenplay from his own stage play.

This movie is not a Cher-fan favorite because the chemistry just isn't there between her and costar Ryan O'Neal, who is about as animated as a popsicle wrapper. Cher turns in a top-notch performance, but the script is a little beneath her and too silly, according to fans.

Ready to Wear (Prêt-à-Porter)
(1994)

Director: Robert Altman.
Cast: Tim Robbins, Julia Roberts, Sophia Loren,
Kim Basinger, Lyle Lovett, Tracey Ullman,
Forest Whitaker, Lili Taylor, Marcello Mastroianni,
Stephen Rea, Danny Aiello, Lauren Bacall, Teri Garr,
Jean-Pierre Cassel, Chiara Mastroianni,
Sally Kellerman, Richard E. Grant, Michel Blanc,
Jean Rochefort, Francois Cluzet, Anouk Aimee,
Christy Turlington, Cher, Harry Belafonte,
Helena Christensen, Thierry Mugler, Issey Miyake,
Elsa Klensch, Jean-Paul Gaultier, Christian Lacroix,
Naomi Campbell, and Sonia Rykiel.

As the fashion world gathers in France for the huge Prêt-à-Porter show, Robert Altman weaves their impossibly self-absorbed stories into a bright, comic fabric in this biting satire. Altman traces a half dozen or more plots, bound by the

mystery surrounding the death of the much-hated head of the fashion council.

The significance of this movie in Cher history is the fact that it was directed by Robert Altman, the famous director friend of her mom's who gave her her big "mainstream movie" break in *Come Back to the Five and Dime, Jimmy Dean, Jimmy Dean*. Altman personally invited Cher to make a cameo as a guest at a European fashion show. Actually, she is really just playing herself. Also of significance to Cher fans is that old friend (and *Sonny & Cher Show* regular) Teri Garr has a small role. On the set, Cher got to meet some of her designer idols, who play themselves in the movie, including Christian LaCroix, Issey Miyake, and Jean-Paul Gaultier.

The Player
(1992)

Director: Robert Altman
Cast: Tim Robbins, Greta Scacchi, Whoopi Goldberg, Brion James, Cynthia Stevenson, and Vincent D'Onofrio.

Studio executive Griffin Mill has been receiving threatening postcards from an unidentified writer. Adding to his pressure is the fact that a hungry young upstart, Larry Levy, is threatening his position as heir apparent at the studio. Attempting to track down the postcard writer, Mill inadvertently kills writer David Kahane (believing him to be the culprit) and now must also fight to stay out of prison and to cope with his own feelings of guilt. Cher has a quick cameo as a guest at a premiere facing the paparazzi's flashes going off in her face. She's in fully glitzy regalia, and it's Cher at her most, well, Cher-ish!

Mermaids
(1990)

Director: Richard Benjamin
Cast: Cher, Bob Hoskins, Winona Ryder, Christina Ricci, Caroline McWilliams, and Betsy Townsend.

Eccentric, constantly moving Mrs. Flax has two daughters in tow: Charlotte, who defies her free spirited, Jewish mother by wanting to become a nun, and Kate, who lovingly supports both her mother and big sister. But their newest town has a secret in store as the two elder Flax women fall unexpectedly in love with two locals. Cher makes an adorable Mrs. Flax, but we can't quite fathom her having an affair with the rather dumpy looking Bob Hoskins, who reportedly had a hard time suppressing his English accent in this role. Cher had a hit with her remake of Betty Everett's "Shoop Shoop (It's in His Kiss)" song from this movie, and admitted that working with offbeat young actresses Christina Ricci and Winona Ryder was a blast. Cher fans loved Mrs. Flax's garish sixties wardrobe and giant falls. The wardrobe items from this movie are very collectible, needless to say.

Moonstruck
(1987)

Director: Norman Jewison
Cast: Cher, Nicolas Cage, Vincent Gardenia,
Danny Aiello, Olympia Dukakis, Julie Bovasso,
and John Mahoney.

Under the magic of the full moon, an Italian-American family tries to sort out their romantic entanglements and find happiness. Tired of being single, and longing for security, widow Loretta Castorini agrees to marry Johnny Cammareri, a man she admittedly doesn't love. While he visits his dying mother in Sicily, she visits his estranged brother Ronny in order to invite him to the wedding, and, much to her surprise, finds herself deeply attracted to him. Loretta's parents have equally complex romantic lives; her father is involved in a long-term affair, while a college professor avidly pursues her mother.

Cher was very critical when she saw the rushes of her first scenes and thought she "stank." Needless to say, she couldn't have been as bad as she thought as she won an Academy Award for her role. Cher has admitted that she picked up a lot of the traits for her moody Italian-American character from what she remembers of Sonny's older relatives.

Suspect
(1987)

Director: Peter Yates
Cast: Cher, Dennis Quaid, Liam Neeson,
John Mahoney, Joe Montegna, Fred Melamed,
Philip Bosco, and Michael Beach.

A courtroom thriller about an exhausted public defender who is saddled with an impossible case: clearing a deaf-mute Vietnam vet vagrant of a murder charge. All the odds seem to be against the defender until one of the jurors, a seductive if rather slippery Washington lobbyist, decides to help her by searching for clues himself. In between bouts of snappy verbal sparring, the unlikely team uncovers a sinister conspiracy.

Cher played the public defender and her costars included the very sexy Dennis Quaid and Liam Neeson. Fans like this movie because it gives them a one-time chance to see their diva dressed in a conservative manner, with much less makeup than usual.

The Witches of Eastwick
(1987)

Director: George Miller
Cast: Cher, Jack Nicholson, Susan Sarandon,
Michelle Pfeiffer, Veronica Cartwright,
Richard Jenkins, and Keith Jochim.

In the tranquil New England town of Eastwick reside three best friends: sexy, dark-haired Alexandra, emotional redhead Jane, and intelligent blond Sukie. Bored and dateless, this trio of divorced "witches" decide to conjure up their perfect man. He arrives in the form of Daryl Van Horn, charismatic, intelligent, and quite literally a "horny little devil." After Daryl easily seduces each witch by tapping into and exploiting her individual needs, the foursome begin living together in communal bliss. But soon the three women realize that Daryl is not the man of their dreams after all, and abandon him. But unfortunately for the lovely trio, hell hath no fury like the Devil scorned!

Cher says this is the film on which she felt the greatest camaraderie with her costars. She was in awe of Michelle Pfeiffer's beauty and Susan Sarandon's talents and off-camera warmth. Cher admits in her nutrition book that she and her costars ate M&Ms and Reese's Pieces in their dressing trailers until her jeans no longer fit. She gained thirteen pounds during the two-month shoot.

Come Back to the 5 & Dime, Jimmy Dean, Jimmy Dean
(1982)

Director: Robert Altman
Cast: Cher, Sandy Dennis, Kathy Bates,
and Karen Black.

Members of the James Dean fan club, which was formed in 1955, hold their twenty-year reunion at a five and dime. The different directions their lives have taken, and the various degrees of success with which they have met, create numerous striking and insightful contrasts. Cher considers this her first "important" movie role, and admits to being initially intimidated by the grand talent in the cast, especially Sandy Dennis.

This film started out as a successful play on Broadway, which was Cher's only foray onto the Great White Way. The movie didn't do that well in terms of box-office sales, but fans still find Cher's outspoken waitress character to be a "classic."

Mask
(1985)

Director: Peter Bogdonovich
Cast: Cher, Eric Stoltz, Sam Elliott,
Richard A. Dysart, Estelle Getty, Laura Dern,
and Micole Mercurio.

Mask was based on the true story of Rocky Dennis, a boy who was born with craniodiaphyseal dysplasia, a fatal disease that causes calcium to accumulate in the skull and makes the head grow to twice normal size. Despite his disease, the sixteen-year-old Rocky just wants to live a normal life with his mom and her biker-gang buddies. His optimistic and fun-loving outlook wins him many friends and supporters, including a beautiful blind girl he meets while working at a summer camp. This film is the first time we get to see Cher in biker garb (she seemed to adopt it for real life wear around this time as well). It also started, for Cher, a lifelong desire to raise money for the Children's Craniofacial Foundation.

Silkwood
(1983)

Director: Mike Nichols
Cast: Meryl Streep, Kurt Russell, Cher,
Craig T. Nelson, and Josef Sommer.

Based on the true story of Karen Silkwood, an employee of an Oklahoma plutonium plant who died in a mysterious car accident before blowing the whistle about dangerous conditions at the plant, the film earned five Academy Award nominations, including Best Director, Best Actress (Meryl Streep), and Best Original Screenplay.

Cher later admitted to being in awe of Meryl Streep's talent and leading man Kurt Russell's old-fashioned chivalry. This film shows Cher as a "real person," with no makeup and usually sporting jeans. It's admirable that she can go from being the ultimate onstage diva to playing a factory worker who's rough around the edges.

It took a lot of guts for Cher to play Silkwood's lesbian lover, Dolly, as there were still not a lot of lesbian characters in the movies at that point in history.

Chastity
(1969)

Director: Alessio de Paola
Cast: Cher, Barbara London, and Stephen Whittaker.

Sonny Bono wrote and produced this starring vehicle for Cher, which nearly made the superstar couple go bankrupt. In the film, Cher plays a sexy, surly, bell-bottomed runaway who gets into all kinds of mischief with the opposite sex, but eventually finds herself in the end.

The movie poster slogan was "What's wrong with Chastity?" and it gave critics free reign to go crazy insulting the film. The M rating did not help in terms of attracting younger fans, which were not allowed into theaters. Despite the film being a flop, a *Time* magazine review read: "Cher is on-screen for virtually the whole film and still handles herself with an easy flair. She clearly enjoys playing a side-of-the-mouth, post-teeny-bopper bitch, and even brings off the role's dark comedy."

Good Times
(1967)

Director: William Friedkin
Cast: Sonny Bono, Cher, and George Sanders

Sonny and Cher, as themselves, contemplate the jump from pop superstardom to the big screen after a big-shot producer makes them an offer they can't refuse. Actually, Sonny can refuse, as he quickly imagines the various possibilities of a Hollywood career, all of which are quite ridiculous. The bulk of the story revolves around Sonny's movie-production fantasies and not so much around Cher. Our favorite diva thinks she was dreadful in the movie because at the time, her heart was not in it. Songs include:

C
H
A
S
T
I
T
Y

"I Got You Babe," "It's the Little Things," "Good Times," "Trust Me," "Don't Talk to Strangers," "I'm Gonna Love You," and "Just a Name."

This movie is fun to watch because it essentially shows Sonny & Cher as themselves, going through their usual Hollywood business and sporting those famous furry vests and Beatle boots. The viewer also gets a taste of the funny Sonny & Cher vignettes that would become so important later in their career on their CBS variety show.

Wild on the Beach
(1965)

Director: Maury Dexter
Cast: Frankie Randall, Sherry Jackson, Jackie & Gayle, Sonny Bono, Cher, The Astronauts, and Sandy Nelson.

This teen music flick is typical sixties fare: girls in bikinis having boy problems, musclemen primping and pumping, and lesser-known teen pop acts including Sandy Nelson (of *Teen Beat* fame) and the Astronauts performing on the beach. It stars the poor man's Frankie Avalon and Annette Funicello, Frankie Randall and Sherry Jackson. Sonny and Cher look out of place on the sand in their fur vests. It's pure, pre-hippie innocent sixties fare and has a high kitsch rating among fans of camp.

CHAPTER ELEVEN

The Top Ten Cher Scandals

Cher is no stranger to controversy and that's perhaps because the show-biz world's eyes have always been upon her. Whether the shock came from her divorcing Sonny and hooking up with Gregg Allman or from calling David Letterman an "a-hole," Cher is the only major celebrity (other than Elizabeth Taylor) the world's been talking about, or if you will, analyzing, for nearly four decades. Many would agree that Cher has remained in the public eye largely due to the media's fascination with her. The press, including the tabloids, seem bent on reporting ever little infraction of her life, partly because of her flair for inventing a larger-than-life persona and her endearing celebrity.

Dozens of faithful fans were queried about what they thought would make up the list of top-ten sensational Cher scandals. The items are listed in order of significance according to fans.

1. Divorce from Sonny

When Cher divorced Sonny in 1975, it was a shock to the world because they appeared to be so caring and loving on the *Sonny & Cher Comedy Hour*. They started and ended each show holding hands and no one except those on the set saw the relationship dissolving. But by the time they divorced, they had lived separate lives for two years in the same Bel Air home, with Sonny moving his personal secretary into his bedroom and Cher taking up a whole different wing of the mansion. Cher claimed not only did Sonny control all her business ventures, but kept her from learning the simpler tasks of life, including writing her

Divorcing Sonny in 1975 shocked America.

own checks. The divorce was bitter, but not bitter enough to prevent them from coming back for a few months to do the *Sonny & Cher Show* together. Sonny and Cher eventually did their own separate shows—Cher's was a hit for one season, while Sonny's was a bomb even before the thirteen weeks were up.

2. Marriage to Gregg Allman

Only ten days after a 1975 quickie wedding in Las Vegas, Cher filed for divorce from rocker Gregg Allman, mainly due to her frustration with his drug use. He promised to clean up and they stayed married for two years, however, they spent only about a quarter of that time together since he was always out on the road. Cher also claims that Gregg left notes late at night claiming he was out at the dentist or the recording studio, but of course, she knew better. Insiders say that in the whole time since the divorce, Gregg has only seen his son, Elijah, about five times.

3. Hooking Up with Rob Camilletti

Cher met her twenty-two-year-old Italian stallion in the early eighties, and after just one night with Camilletti, Cher was impressed with both his classic Italian looks and how he seemed like what she called a 1940s kind of man. The relationship ended after a few years when Cher allegedly caught her golden boy in bed with a porn star. (That's what a tabloid reported).

Cher has always despised the "bagel boy" moniker Rob Camilletti received in the tabloids. After all, he was a young aspiring actor when they first met.

4. Lori Davis Haircare Product Commercials

Cher claimed doing this series of late-night infomercials in 1990 was the "smarmiest" thing she had ever done in her career. She claims that when friend and Los Angeles hair-product guru Lori Davis asked her to appear on spots promoting her shampoos, conditioners, and styling products, she had no idea that the spots would be on every network twenty-four hours a day. Cher attests this kept her from getting movie offers for a couple of years.

5. The "If I Could Turn Back Time" Video

This is arguably Cher's most outrageous on-screen escapade ever, even if it was on the small screen. Since our favorite diva was scantily clad with her entire derriere exposed for the world to see and with a front piece that required the most intricate Brazilian bikini wax ever, the normally liberal MTV executive staff demanded it only be shown at night after 9 P.M. The cheering sailors seemed to make the video a little more scandalous than it really was. Whether you like the video or not, it made the song Cher's first Top Ten hit in many years. The risqué outfit became the all-time most popular getup with Cher impersonators, a couple of whom she later brought onstage with her for her *Heart of Stone* concert tour.

6. Her Relationship with Warren Beatty

In 1998, Cher admitted that she had dated famous Hollywood lothario Warren Beatty in 1962, just after getting her driver's license. She was sixteen at the time. One day over the phone, Cher's mom, Georgia, told Warren her daughter's real age (Cher had lied), but Cher says that seemed to have made him like her more! Beatty has never made a public comment about his relationship with the Dark Lady.

Since the seventies, sensational headlines have always followed Cher.

7. Suing Sonny's Estate for Back Alimony

In 2000, Cher sued Sonny's estate for a million dollars in back alimony, but no reason was given to the press except that it had been "owed" to her for years. Sonny was only worth a couple of million when he died, and Sonny fans felt that Cher was taking advantage of his estate. As of mid 2002, there was no word as to whether this matter has been settled. It's no secret that Cher would want this delicate issue kept out of the papers as much as possible.

8. Average White Band Overdose Scandal

Back when Cher was partying in Hollywood circa September 1973 and her relationship with Sonny was coming to an end, she was allegedly dating Alan Gorrie, a member of the Scottish funk-pop group Average White Band. After a two-week run at the Troubadour, two members of the group overdosed on strychnine-laced heroin at a Hollywood Hills party, and Cher was responsible for walking Alan around and saving his life.

9. Freaking Out When Chastity "Came Out"

When Chastity came out, Cher admits she did not handle it well. Although she has always been around gay people, when she heard her own daughter was homosexual via a phone call from Sonny, she freaked out. Cher acknowledged that she always thought her daughter was a "tomboy" who would "outgrow" that phase. She sulked about her daughter's confession for months. Now, claims Cher, Chastity and her girlfriend stay over at Mom's Malibu house and she is glad that her daughter has found someone who makes her happy. In 1998, Chastity wrote a book on the subject titled *Family Outing*, and who but Mom would have penned the foreword?

10. Calling David Letterman an A-Hole on the Air

When Letterman's staff did not pick up her $38,000 Morgan Hotel bill as promised before she came on the program, she called him an "a-hole" on the air. (She was not paid for her appearance.) The late-night host was supposedly peeved by this for a month. Letterman and Cher have since made up. A few weeks after Cher's appearance on the show, Shirley MacLaine came on and said jokingly, "You know, Cher said you were an a-hole, and you are."

Believe what you will, but only Cher knows the truth.

There's always something interesting to say about Cher.

CHAPTER TWELVE

What People Say About Cher

"I am such a big fan because there is nobody on the planet like her."   —Oprah Winfrey

"Part of my mother is very much the insider. The other part is the outsider. But I never worry about her. She is a survivor and a fighter."

—Chastity Bono

"Cher is something. I don't know what it is. Maybe it's the ability to make people feel. And maybe to do that, you have to experience a lot of pain, like Cher has." —Georgia Holt (Cher's mother)

"Cher has never been a real secure person. She's a magnificent talent, but complicated."

—Sonny Bono

"When we design costumes for her, it has nothing to do with fashion. It has nothing to do with anything but the fact that we are attempting to present to the world this creature in her own right."

—Bob Mackie

"Cher is one of those rare entertainers who has no private face that is contrary to her public one. What you see with her is what you get . . . she has never tried to impress with her wit, or her humor, or her looks. She just IS. How she feels on any given day is how she presents herself. Take it or leave it, that has always been her motto.

—J. Randy Taraborrelli, author of *Cher*

Sonny: "Cher needed a husband, a father, a brother, a lover, everything. I loved giving it."

"I am a huge Cher fan! I just think she's just fantastic! She was a strong representative for the women's movement." —Linda Blair, actress

"She was a blend of different cultures, and she kind of popularized the exoticness of a lot of those different cultures fashionwise, in her songs, and ultimately, in the '80s and '90s, in the characters she's played on the silver screen."
—Mark Bego, author of *Cher: If You Believe*

"We think of her as the epitome of the American woman." —*Vogue* magazine

"When I met Cher, I knew she was going to be great. I thought she was a flower that hadn't blossomed yet, but when she did, the whole world would know it." —Sonny Bono

With Chastity. "My mom wasn't exactly like the other kids' moms. She didn't look like June Cleaver."

"There is no one like Cher in the entertainment business. I don't care if she has been completely re-created by a plastic surgeon . . . or not . . . she's still magic, and I say, God bless the child. She's one of the few things that have been consistent in our lives during insane times and, for that alone, I think she should be greatly valued."
—J. Randy Taraborrelli, author of *Cher*

"Cher is one of the most talented women I've ever met. She's got depth and emotion that haven't even been touched."
—Peter Bogdanovich, director of *Mask*

"Cher is still a simple girl who longs to live a happy, simple life. It's true she always wanted to be a famous star, but I don't think she bargained for the high cost of it." —Georgia Holt

"I expected her to be strong and sure of herself. But she's not. There's the Cher that people see every day, but I see a shy, wide-eyed little girl."
—Rob Camilletti

"Cher has the best armpits in the business! No one in the business has her ease." —Bob Mackie

"What struck me when we met was how different she is in private life from the public image of her. She is like everyone else. Cher is very real. Very honest." —Meryl Streep, *Silkwood* costar

"Cher took herself from a silly young girl with a famous belly button to become what she wanted to be. And she did it her way." —Barbara Walters

"Oh God, what a body!" —Bob Mackie

"She is actually dedicated to her work. She's a homebody, too. She values what we all value—friends, family, hanging out playing board games at home."
—Georgeanne LaPierre, Cher's half-sister

Cher and Rob Camelletti, circa late eighties.

"She has guts. If Cher says she's going to do something, she will do it." —Robert Altman

"I was madly in love with Cher, even though I've been living 50 percent of the time before her as a gay man. She knew everything about me because I told her." —David Geffen

"Cher started the square-nail look. She wanted something different and I said, 'What the hell different can you do with nails?' Take off the round and we figured leave them blunt."—Minnie Smith, Cher's manicurist in the seventies

Cher backstage with sis, Georgeanne, in 1990.

"Having sat next to Cher and interviewing her one-on-one, I have a strong picture of what Cher is like when the cameras are not rolling. She is frank. She is outspoken. She is compassionate, and very opinionated. Cher is a media star of legendary proportions, yet, she is very down to earth. She is not afraid to speak her mind. In other words, Cher is everything I had hoped and imagined she would be."—Mark Bego, author of *Cher: If You Believe*

"I'm not into my mom's whole fame thing. I don't ever want to be like, crazy famous."
—Elijah Blue Allman

"Despite everything, I still love the Sonny & Cher act. The hardest part for me was to learn how to separate myself from it. Cher always said to me, 'take us to the top.' I thought that was the role she wanted me to play. You've got to give someone like Cher a lot of credit. She's worked very hard to get where she is. I can't take that away from her." —Sonny Bono

"Cher is an instinctive actress. She has that rare honesty which is so surprising since her image has always been in boldface." —Meryl Streep

"Cher is the epitome of a diva. She's strong, beautiful, and knows what she wants. She just keeps changing with the times." —Liv Tyler

"On 1971's the *Sonny & Cher Comedy Hour*, Cher plays not the dutiful and doting wife of old, but rather the sassy feminist ready to give her husband a dig rather than fetch him a beer. From tart-tongued feminist wife waging an early skirmish in the battle of the sexes, to working mother, to finally sexy divorcee going it alone, Cher was, in many ways, the personification of the seventies." —Danny Bonaduce

Since Cher's appearances on *Will & Grace*, she and Sean Hayes, who portrays "Jack"—Cher's biggest fan—have become great friends in real life.

"She was a sweetheart. I thought she was going to be a problem because she's Cher and she's a big star. But she was one of the best people I've ever worked with—such a caring, nice human being. I can't say enough about Cher."
—Paolo Seganti, actor in *Tea With Mussolini*

The Cher Illusion

Heidi Thompson

Cher is one of the most impersonated celebrities in the world, not just by drag queens, but by female performers as well. One of the top leading female impersonators in the country is Heidi Thompson, and she's really a she! Thompson, who naturally resembles the legendary diva, has been hailed the "premiere Cher" impersonator by national press as well as various sources of television entertainment. Thompson's portrayal of Cher has elicited various responses from reviewers, ranging from "uncanny" to "unbelievable" to even "scary." Her stunning illusion of Cher doesn't end with the famous look either— Thompson's vocal accuracy is right on the mark and her diva "Cher-like attitude" and wit couldn't be even more precise. Thompson has been performing as Cher in full costume for more than twelve years, first in the famed Legends in Concert at the Imperial Palace Hotel and later at the American Superstars Show, both in Las Vegas.

"I started out with my own Las Vegas lounge act in which I did impressions of various artists and one of those impressions was of Cher," she explained. "The producer of the largest impersonator show in the world called Legends in Concert in Las Vegas saw my act and asked me to play Cher in his show." Thompson now performs for the corporate market, leaving more time to work on other projects as a writer of scripts for television, film, and stage.

How does one prepare to become Cher is a question she is often asked. "Well, I've been doing it for so long that all I have to do now is put on the costume and warm up my voice," she said. "As soon as the wig goes on my head, Cher automatically appears. It's just like that. I can do several other celebrity impressions and I have my own original comedy characters, but I chose not to do anymore serious impersonations because the Cher character takes up so much of my time."

The highlight of her act includes an audience participation in which Thompson bring an unsuspecting male onto the stage and places a Sonny Bono wig on him and together they sing "I Got You Babe." Thompson is capable of portraying the Cher from the seventies to the present, and that entails a lot of costume and wig changes for one, one hour show.

"I'll do three decades of Cher looks and sing 'After All,' 'Bang Bang,' 'Believe,' 'Dark Lady,' 'Gypsies, Tramps and Thieves,' 'If I Could Turn Back Time,' 'I Found Someone,' 'Strong Enough,' 'The Way of Love,' and others as a regular song list. Since I have dozens of different wigs and costumes, I am able to provide whatever is requested."

Of all the eras of Cher to perform, Thompson says she enjoys being the eighties Cher the best because of the star's big hair days, the rock image she presented, and, of course, for songs like "If I Could Turn Back Time."

When Nickelodeon's new television network TV Land premiered, Thompson went on the road as Cher to promote the reruns of the *Sonny & Cher Comedy Hour*. Since then she has appeared as Cher on other television shows like *The Nanny* and the *Leeza Gibbons Show*. "I've had many highlights in my career and starring on *The Nanny* as Cher recovering from plastic surgery is one of them. Fran Drescher said to me, 'I can't tell you how many people thought you were really Cher!' On the show my face was bandaged up so all that was used was my voice and body language. My singing voice was also used for a female impersonator of Cher to lip-sync to 'Bang Bang.' It was a lot of fun and a great experience for me."

When the Vegas-based entertainer isn't portraying Cher, she is working on her screenplay and involved in Scientology and Dianetics. Thompson is a spiritual person who believes in using her artistic talents to help others in as many creative ways as possible.

Heidi Thompson

as

Cher

Wayne Smith

Wayne Smith is one of those rare entertainers that not only makes you smile, but also dazzles you with his natural vibrancy and knows how to make you feel as if he is performing just for you. While Smith is considered one of America's leading Cher impersonators, he is also known for his many other character adaptations such as Marilyn Monroe and Dolly Parton.

"I owe a lot to Cher because I have been able to make a very good living impersonating her," said Smith, who hails from Dallas, Texas. "For as long as I can remember, I have been a Cher fan for so long because I think she is extremely talented and beautiful." Smith was a hit at the first annual Cher Convention 2000 in Chicago. He performed several songs as the "Cher of the eighties" and conducted a seminar for fans to learn more about what it takes to transform into Cher.

Smith has an interesting background since he once worked for Bob Mackie doing the marking on the incredible creations that the famed designer would dream up. Smith also helped with fringe beading on the outfit Cher wore when she won her Academy Award. "I have so many memories of those times, one is doing the beaded fringe for Cher's gown she wore when she won her Academy Award. "I made the beaded fringe on my bed at home at night," he recalled, "so I feel very close to Cher in that instance.

Smith has been performing live since the eighties when he won first place and a thousand dollars for being the best Marilyn Monroe at a Halloween party. He was then asked to audition his "Marilyn" act for a show at a nightclub called La Cage Aux Follies. He also did Dolly Parton.

"The first show I did was at the Fontainebleau Hilton in Miami, Florida," he said. "I was there for one year, after which I went on to perform at the infamous La Cage in Hollywood for six years. I always wanted to impersonate Cher, but it was not even something that the producer thought could be done well. I proved him wrong when I auditioned Cher for him one night and the crowd loved it."

Needless to say, Smith replaced Dolly Parton with Cher. "I always knew I could do Cher. She influences my life daily. When I'm performing, there isn't a day that goes by I don't hear someone yell, 'Hey Cher!' " Smith's rave reviews attest that he is a most convincing Cher. As the Associated Press wrote: "Wayne Smith is second only to Cher."

1998 fave Cher Convention impersonator Wayne Smith turns back time for a much delighted and captive audience.

WAYNE SMITH
AS

Preparing to be Cher these days is a piece of cake for Smith. "Since I sing and talk as Cher in shows, it comes naturally to me now. I love to listen to her songs while I makeup, it seems to help. It takes roughly about one hour to do the makeup, and then the wig and costume, and Cher is 'in the building.' People are always amazed that I sing live and can actually talk just like her, too. I always hear people say you even laugh like Cher."

Smith, who is accustomed to performing in casinolike venues across the country, was apprehensive about appearing at the legend at the first annual Cher Convention in Chicago. "I was very nervous meeting and performing for the die-hard fans," he explained. "My first song was 'After All,' and when I started to sing it, I was backstage. I came through the door with the white fur coat that was copied from Cher's *Heart of Stone* tour. The fans went wild, which made me so happy, I finally got the acceptance that I hoped for. The Cher fans made me so proud."

Most of Smith's costumes are designed and made with the help of the women who do the beading for Bob Mackie. Many of the gowns are replicas of costumes Cher has worn. His wigs have to be special-ordered, too, and the manufacturers have discontinued several of his favorites. "I'm always looking for what will work best as Cher," Smith related. "Many of the other items I use are either made or bought from many different places. I always seem to find things for 'Cher,' more than for Wayne. But, hey, that's okay, too."

In the future, Smith hopes for the golden opportunity to perform with his idol. "I know that is a big and almost impossible goal, but I was always told by my father to aim big, and that's big. Who knows, maybe it will happen at a future Cher Convention. I'm ready for it. Now that would be a dream come true."

Like Cher, Smith, too, is involved with the Children's Craniofacial Association. He wrote a book titled *Starbabies: The Untold Story of Falling Stars*, and donates a portion of the proceeds to CCA. While it is hard to predict what Wayne Smith will do next, no doubt it is sure to bring many more smiles and memories to those Cher fans whose lives he has touched along the way.

"I really think that Cher fans are one of a kind. They have to pull for someone who isn't always on everyone's 'favorite' list. Cher is a rebel and does what she feels and her fans take a lot of flack for it."

—Wayne Smith, Cher impersonator

"The times were really changing around 1970 and women's lib was coming in. Women were assuming more of a dominant role, not only in television, but in real life, and I think that this opened up the possibilities for Cher to zing in those one-liners and be the one that's the smarter of the two."—Mark Bego, author of *Cher: If You Believe*

"Look at how many careers she's had. She is a chamelon."

—David Geffen

Cyndi Lauper opened for Cher's Believe Tour.

Cher will always be at the top of her game because she projects an incredible sense of honesty and a larger-than-life appeal, and she possesses enormous talent that cannot be harnessed.

Selected Songs Written by Sonny Bono and Recorded by Sonny & Cher and by Cher

From the early sixties to the mid-seventies, Sonny Bono wrote a good portion of the Sonny & Cher, solo Cher, and solo Sonny songs. This is an abbreviated list of the more popular ones.

Sonny & Cher

"Baby Don't Go" (1965)

"I Got You Babe" (1965)

"Walkin' the Quetzal" (1965)

"Sing C'est Vie" (1965)

"It's Gonna Rain" (1965)

"Just You" (1965)

"But You're Mine" (1966)

"I Look for You" (1966)

"The Revolution Kind" (1967)

"The Beat Goes On" (1967)

"Have I Stayed Too Long" (1967)

"Monday" (1967)

"Love Don't Come" (1967)

"Podunk" (1967)

"Little Man" (1967)

"Living for You" (1967)

"It's the Little Things" (1967)

"Good Times" (1967)

"Trust Me" (1967)

"Don't Talk to Strangers" (1967)

"Just a Name" (1967)

"A Beautiful Story" (1967)

"Hello" (1967)

"You're a Friend of Mine" (1969)

"I Would Marry You Today" (1969)

"A Cowboy's Work Is Never Done" (1972)

"Somebody" (1972)

"Mama Was a Rock and Roll Singer, and Papa Used to Write All Her Songs (Part 1 & 2)" (1973)

Sonny Solo
(from Inner Views album)

"I Just Sit There" (1967)

"I Told My Girl to Go Away" (1967)

"My Best Friend's Girl Is Out of Sight" (1967)

"Pammie's on a Bummer" (1967)

Cher Solo

"Needles and Pins" (with Jack Nitzche) (1965)

"See See Rider" (with Green/Stone) (1965)

"Dream Baby" (1965)

"Bang Bang (My Baby Shot Me Down)" (1965)

"Where Do You Go" (1965)

"Magic in the Air (I Feel Something)" (1966)

"You Better Sit Down Kids" (1968)

"But I Can't Love You More" (1968)

"Mama (When My Dollies Have Babies)" (1968)

"She's No Better Than Me" (1969)

"Don't Put It on Me" (1971)

"Classified 1A" (1971)

"The First Time" (1972)

CHAPTER THIRTEEN

Cher Speaks Out

Cher is outspoken on everything from her career to her personal life and back again. But unlike celebrities who seem to have rehearsed answers to interviewers' questixons, Cher seems to always have a fresh approach, even if it's a question she's answered a thousand times. Cher has the great ability to laugh at herself and the entertainment field as a whole, which has always made her a much sought-after target of the media.

Cher's favorite topics for discussion include her music, her movies, her children, fashion (no surprise), and her days with Sonny, and what she thinks about men. Even though she is known privately as a deeply emotional person, Cher comes off as a levelheaded and honest woman in interviews. Perhaps it is when Cher is speaking of the love for her children that she seems the most glowing. She is beyond grateful that her fans have followed her over four decades of career ups-and-downs and personal highs and lows. Cher's deep love for her fans is echoed the loudest not in her quotes though, but in the fact that she thanks each and every fan that asks for her autograph.

So read on for Cher's most interesting and revealing quotes. As time as goes on and her celebrity continues to grow to meet a new generation of admirers, Cher becomes even more honest and open about herself. You never know what's going to come out of Cher's mouth, but you can bet she's going to say something incredibly fascinating and equally as honest. This ultimate survivor tells it like it is!

"You can stand up for what you do, but it's really difficult to stand up for what you don't do."

On Her Sixties Fame

"I remember that time as being a lot of work. Sonny and I were never around rock-and-roll people because Sonny didn't like going out. He didn't dance and didn't want to anything, so my life was my work."

"I'm my own woman, and I have to do the things I want to do with my life."

On Being Famous

"I just wanted to be famous. Maybe not with a specific talent, but as a personality."

"Most famous people would be devastated if it all stopped. There's the odd occasion when people are following you or trying to shoot pictures of you in the bathroom and you go 'Fuck off, I don't want this. It's not worth it!' But the truth is once you've had it, it's like part of you, it would be like losing your arm. I've been famous since I was like eighteen, so it's all I've ever known as an adult."

On Leaving Sonny

"People ask me if I left Sonny for another man. I tell them no, I left him for another woman—me. I didn't stop loving Son. All of sudden, I just didn't want to be his wife anymore. I could never stop loving Sonny. It was Sonny who let me become 'Cher.' It was all through Sonny. That's how it happened—through Sonny."

"I'm my own woman, and I have to do the things I want to do with my life. What I am doing is growing up for the very first time in my life, and like everyone else who's growing up, I'll make mistakes."

On Growing Up

"When I was a kid, I was convinced God had sent me to be an angel. I was the all-time heroine, the super Good Person."

"I was poor when I grew up and I couldn't bear that. My growing up being really poor colors so much of who I am today. I still feel like the same person I was at six years old. I can just buy more things. Because I didn't have stability growing up, I'll probably never get enough of it."

"When I was little, I wanted to be famous. I didn't know what it was going to be, I just wanted to be famous. And when I was famous, I just wanted to be good at something."

On the International Craniofacial Association

"There are all kinds of worthwhile charities. But I can't spread myself too thin. I have to feel committed. If you look at one of these children, knowing that the only thing that keeps them from living a normal, happy, productive life in society is money, it seems a shame."

On Her Appearance Offstage

"I go around grubby all the time; I just don't have the patience, except when I'm working, to put on makeup or look good."

On the Public's Perception of Her

"I've always lived quietly. It's just that when I'm out, I am really out. People think I'm sort of a madwoman, but you know what? I'm really very boring."

On Singing

"From the time I could talk, I began to sing. Singing just came from the inside—something I'd do without thinking whenever I felt good or was really blue."

"When I'm singing, I think it's great," she explains. "It's a wonderful feeling—opening your mouth to sing and this big voice comes out. When I'm on stage I feel like I'm about twenty feet tall. My voice rattles around in my chest like a force and it's so big it fills a whole arena, but then I listen to it on record and it's never as good."

"I like singing what I like, and there are ballads that I still want to do."

On Men

"A girl can wait for the right man to come along, but in the meantime that still doesn't mean she can't have a wonderful time with all the wrong ones."

"I like to have someone I can touch and squeeze and kiss. But I don't fold up and die if I don't have a man around."

"I'm not attracted to guys because they look great. I hardly ever see men that I am attracted to. Then there's the problem of being Cher. It's easy for women to hang out with men that are famous. But no man wants to be Mr. Cher."

"I think men are fun and nice. I don't think they are necessary to live."

On the Decisions She Makes in Life

"I answer to two people, myself and God."

On Winning the Academy Award

"It is an honor to be nominated, but the moment you don't win, you're a loser; so you go there as a nominee and everyone's going, 'Oh congratulations, it's great.' And then when you lose, people kinda shy away from you. It's like they are embarrassed. They don't want to talk to you and you just kinda find yourself wanting to sneak out of the building."

"I don't think this means I am somebody, but I guess I'm on my way."

"No matter how much I achieve, I always feel like an outsider."

On Sonny's Funeral

"Sonny was the most unforgettable character I ever met."

On Her Staying Power

"Ya know, I saw a joke once that said the only things that will be left after a nuclear holocaust will be the roaches and Cher."

"Some years I'm the coolest thing that ever happened, and then the next year, everybody is so over me, and I'm just so past my sell date. I am constantly surprised by any success I have."

On Her Music

"I am absolutely egotistical."

"Music emotionally strikes a chord. But to sing something, you don't actually have to be living it.

"I take chances. What else can I do? If you don't keep growing, you will die. If my option was just rolling out the same old thing, I'd never step into a studio again."

I don't listen to my own music. If we're going to do a show someone else will come up with copies of all the old stuff so I can relearn the songs. The fun of it is doing it, not listening back to it."

"Music does everything. It hits you in a place that you don't have to process. I think music bypasses all those intellectual processes. When something hits you, it hits you in that place right in your chest, that place right in the middle of your body where you take in things that don't go near your head."

On Her Career Moves

"I've always taken risks. I never worried what the world might really think of me."

"I keep hoping I'm going to catch that Frank Sinatra wave and never have to prove myself again."

"People always go, that's it for her, and I guess someday it's gonna be 'it.' But so far it hasn't been."

On Why She Married Greg Allman

"I don't know why I married Gregory. I felt so controlled by Sonny. I knew Greg couldn't control himself, much less try to control me. He also had one of the sweetest personalities I've ever seen."

Despite her colorful persona, Cher says: "It's harder for me to walk in a room with five people than to walk onstage in front of twenty-five thousand. I've always been really shy."

119

On Her Cosmetic Surgery

"I think this about plastic surgery, it's my body. Women should be given a choice, like with abortion. If I wanna put my tits on my back, they're mine."

"People seem to pick on me more than anybody else. Cosmetic surgery gives me a lift and a little more security."

On the Cher Show

"When I first started the series, I was scared to death. It was like leaving home and going out on your own for the first time."

On Rob Camilletti

"My relationship with Rob was the best. He was so much fun. I felt that I was in really good hands when I was with him. We are still the best of friends."

On Her Fans

"What I do, I do for myself and my fans, the new ones and the die-hard ones. The other people, the critics, what they say is like the poison of the business. But you have to take that along with the good. I think my fans have been unbelievable, because they just stuck by me when it looked like I was dead to the world and never coming back."

On Wanting to be a Grandmother

"Hey, I could have been a grandmother years ago. Oh, I would love it! Oh, yes. I would love that more than anything. Is the world ready . . . Like, I care?"

On Love

"If you don't love, what else is left for you? I don't think you ever give up on love. You see it everywhere. It's the most powerful emotion there is."

On Emotional Pain

"Pain is not the worst thing that can happen to you. When your life is going perfectly, no one stops and goes, 'What can I learn from this?' You really only grow when you face things that make you stop and look at life."

On Whether Her Kids Think She's Cool

"I think I'm cool, but I am sooo uncool to my children. I'm, like, so corny. I embarrass them to no end."

On Sonny

"Sonny didn't like me much when we first met. He liked my best friend, who I lived with at the time. So he moved next door to us. Then I had to move out and Sonny said, 'You can move in with me, just keep the place clean.' I told my mom I was living with a stewardess. When she came to visit, I would throw Son's clothes out the window. He said I lost most of his clothes in the street."

"I'll never forget it. The first time I saw Sonny I swear to God, this has never happened before. Everything went like a star filter around him and there was only him standing there. He wasn't much to look at, but he had this long hair and he was dressed like I had never seen before. He had something."

On Reinventing Herself

"I've had so many rebirths, I should come with my own midwife by now."

On Ever Falling in Love Again

"I can absolutely see myself falling in love again. But I can't imagine why I would ever get married."

"Who knows? I could walk out of my house tomorrow and meet Mr. Right. It always happens when you least expect it."

On Her Music

"I'm not the best singer in the world. I can't listen to my voice. I don't like it. You see all your mistakes when you hear your voice. You see all the imperfections."

On Her Critics

"Sometimes the critics just try to be cute or try to make a name for themselves. There are so many silly things that go into it that you don't know what the fuck they're trying to do."

On Marriage

"Husbands are like fires—they go out when they're left unattended."

On Touring

"People say 'How can you stand a whole summer on the road with all of the one-night gigs?' Well, I thrive on it."

On Her Children

I'm the first person my children call when in a crisis. I'm proud of them both."

On Making Movies

"It's bizarre. I couldn't become an actress for five years because I was a singer. Then everyone was worried that people weren't going to accept me as a singer because I'm an actress. It's very funny."

On Her Looks

"Am I obsessed with the way I look? Do you know what I'd like to say to that? I don't give a flying fuck."

"At home, in the comfort of my own four walls and I'll wear sweat pants and a T-shirt, a sweatshirt over that, my suede boots with a fleece lining, hair up in a ponytail, and no makeup.

I'm clean but ratty. It's such a luxury to be able to slob out like that. Sometimes the simplest thing is the most exciting."

On How She Wants to Be Remembered

"Okay, I was this kid that came from the Valley, not particularly talented in any way. She could sing and dance a little and be funny. But she had something and went on to be successful in everything she endeavored."

On How She Sees Herself in the Future

"I think I would be a cool old lady. Just an older version of myself."

"I have done so much more than I thought I would do, and yet I am not finished."

CHAPTER FOURTEEN

Cher Trivia—
Including the Ultimate Quiz

So, you claim you're such a huge Cher fan that you even know the titles of songs she recorded with Sonny under the names of Caesar & Cleo. And you swear you know the names of all of Cher's romantic partners? That's impressive—but we think we can stump you. If you answer 80 percent of these questions correctly, however, you will win our private, Dark Lady Award.

Questions

1. What was the date that the *Sonny & Cher Comedy Hour* premiered on television?

2. What is the one thing that Cher is "scared to death" of becoming?

3. What prompted Cher to wear wigs in public?

4. Does Cher believe there's a secret to her success?

5. Which Cher video was restricted to night play on MTV because of her rather revealing outfit?

6. True or false: Cher has had work done on her teeth.

7. What year did Cher meet Sonny Bono?

8. What year was Cher's big hit "Bang Bang (My Baby Shot Me Down)" released?

9. Where was Cher born?

10. In 1999, in which MTV-Award category was Cher nominated for the "Believe" video?

11. What is Cher's astrological sign?

12. Who is Elijah Blue's father?

13. True or false: The song "One by One" appears on Cher's *Believe* album.

14. How has Cher used the Oscar she won for *Moonstruck*?

15. In which movie do Cher's half-sister, Georgeanne, and Rob Camilletti make cameo appearances?

16. Cher had a dog while growing up. What was its name?

17. When Cher left home, she went out and got her first tattoo. What was it and where did she put it?

18. In what year did Cher make her film debut?

19. True or false: Cher is dyslexic.

20. Which role was Cher offered in the 1991 hit *Thelma and Louise*?

21. Cher scored number-one hits two times in her life. Name the songs.

22. How many Golden Globe awards has Cher won?

23. True or false: Cher was named one of *People* magazine's Best Dressed in 1999.

24. Which clothing designer is synonymous with Cher's outrageous award-show outfits?

25. Name Cher's character in *Suspect*.

26. How long were Gregg Allman and Cher married before they separated?

27. Did Cher finish high school?

Cher had the body of a model in the seventies: "wonderful torso, shoulders, and back. It's a joy to dress her," Bob Mackie stated.

28. Which of Cher's popular boyfriends was unfairly nicknamed by the press?

29. Did Cher ever suffer from stage fright?

30. How many times has Cher's mother been married?

31. True or false: Cher and Warren Beatty once dated.

32. In which one of Cher's films did she work with Olympia Dukakis?

33. What is one of Cher's all-time favorite sixties songs? (Hint: It was a big hit for Procol Harum)

34. What was Cher's real last name before she married Sonny?

35. In the movie *Goodtimes*, what animal featured was really Sonny and Cher's house pet?

36. What facial feature does Cher consider to be her best?

It's not unusual for a performer of Cher's status to attach a "rider" to her concert contract. A contract rider is what the artist needs—or in some cases, absolutely demands—in order to complete an appearance in concert. Though Cher has many that are fairly reasonable, some stipulations may seem a little extreme. This list does not include all the diva's needs, nor is it in any kind particular order. Does it change how you feel about Cher—or does it make you love her even more!!

Ten of Cher's Concert Contract Demands

1. A wig room.
2. Several bottles of Evian bottled water.
3. Two cube-shaped boxes of aloe Kleenex tissues.
4. A dozen Solo cups that have to be red.
5. A bowl of plain M&Ms.
6. Flowers, but only casa blanca lilies or gardenias.
7. Two couches—one a three-seater, the other a two-seater.
8. A television with a VCR and cable hookup.
9. A large, separate room for a massage table.
10. Two bottles of imported wine—red and white.

37. What nationality is Cher's natural father?
38. True or false: Cher keeps several cats, dogs, and snakes as pets.
39. What was the date that Sonny and Cher legally married?
40. How much money did the 1999 single "Believe" earn in sales?
41. What is the full name of the character Cher portrayed in *Mermaids*?
42. What did Cher pay for the famous Bob Mackie–designed, translucent feathered-and-bugle-beaded dress, as featured on the cover of a 1975 issue of *Time* magazine?
43. What was the date that Sonny and Cher legally divorced?
44. Cher created her Laverne character in the *Sonny & Cher Comedy Hour*. What characteristic of Laverne has Cher said brought the character to life?
45. Name the song that Cher sings on the *Glory of Gershwin* album with Larry Adler.
46. Cher was a guest vocalist on what Gene Simmons song in 1978?
47. What Cher album cover featured an illustration that was later changed to a photograph in its second print run?
48. In what album did Cher write a dedication to Sonny stating: "This album is dedicated with love to Sonny Bono?"
49. In 1965, Cher recorded the Sonny Bono–written "Dream Baby." What name did she use to record the single?
50. To whom was Cher referring when she said "I traded one short ugly man for another."

Answers

1. August 1, 1971.

2. Poor. "I grew up poor and will always feel poor."

3. During the filming of *Mask*, a hair colorist nearly ruined Cher's hair by dying it. Cher decided to never let her real hair be compromised for the roles she plays.

4. Honesty. "I wouldn't be able to sing these songs had I not had heartbreak in my life. I sing them from experience."

5. "If I Could Turn Back Time."

6. True. She had to have her braces taken off and put back on a number of times due to movies and public appearances.

7. 1963.

8. 1966.

9. El Centro, California.

10. The "Best Dance Video" category.

11. Taurus.

12. Gregg Allman.

13. False: "One by One" appears on *Its a Man's World*.

14. As a doorstop, but not anymore.

15. *If These Walls Could Talk*.

16. Blackie.

17. She had a butterfly tattooed on her butt.

18. In 1965, with Sonny, in the film *Wild on the Beach*.

19. True. She was diagnosed at age thirty.

20. Thelma.

21. "I've Got You Babe" in 1965 and "Believe" in 1999.

22. Two—one for *The Sonny & Cher Comedy Hour* and one for *Silkwood*.

23. False—she was named on the Worst Dressed list.

24. Bob Mackie.

25. Kathleen Riley.

26. Nine days.

27. No.

28. Rob Camilletti.

29. Yes.

30. Eight.

31. True.

32. *Moonstruck*.

33. "A Whiter Shade of Pale."

34. Sarkisian.

35. The dog.

36. Her eyes.

37. Armenian.

38. False: Cher only has cats and dogs.

39. October 27, 1969.

40. Over four million dollars.

41. Rachael Flax.

42. Five thousand dollars.

43. June 27, 1975.

44. Chewing gum.

45. "It Ain't Necessarily So."

46. "Living in Sin."

47. *Heart of Stone*.

48. The 1987 self-titled *Cher*.

49. Cherilyn.

50. She traded Sonny Bono for David Geffen.

For this book, dozens of Cher fans were polled via the Internet to see what career projections they had for Cher. These Top five suggestions came up the most and are listed in order of popularity. In addition to this list, and this is a given, many fans would really like to own a complete set of all the old *Sonny & Cher Comedy Hour/ Show* as well as *Cher* solo television and special shows on video and/or DVD.

Top Five Projections for Cher

1. For Warner Brothers Records to release the 1975 *Stars* album on CD. This has been a longtime fan favorite. In fact, hundreds from various on-line Cher groups have gotten together to petition Warner Brothers to release the album on CD.

2. For Cher to produce a compilation video or DVD featuring a complete set of all her music videos to date.

3. For Cher to make another movie and win an Oscar for it.

4. For Cher to record an "original" tribute song to Sonny, or one that combines both their voices like the Natalie Cole and the late Nat King Cole's "Unforgettable." Song choices could include Sonny's solo written recordings "Laugh at Me" and "The Revolution Kind."

5. For Cher to record a Christmas CD.

Old reruns of the *Sonny & Cher Comedy Hour* and *The Cher Show* can occasionally be seen on cable TV's Nick at Nite and TV Land.

Fascinating Facts on Cher

What sets Cher apart from the rest of the pop divas who started out in the mid-sixties is that she is still a viable force on the music scene, while the rest have been relegated to the "oldies" circuit.

When Cher hooked up with Sonny Bono in 1963, she was a sixteen-year-old girl looking for a break in the music business; decades later, she is the ultimate independent woman, someone who has carved her own unique niche in both the pop and acting worlds.

In the seventies, Cher had her own show and served as pop culture's hippie princess and clever, off-the-cuff, hip comedienne. Her interesting choices in men, usually younger musician types, were the talk of the town as much as her outrageous and revealing clothing.

In the eighties, Cher became an Academy Award winner for her role in *Moonstruck* and has gotten meaty roles ever since. She also became a fitness guru, the face behind a fragrance, and specialty-item merchandiser with her goth-inspired Sanctuary catalog. But the best was yet to come for the Dark Lady.

Fans were most amazed when Cher's 1999 dance single "Believe" put her back at the top of the charts after nearly a fifteen-year absence from the Top ten. As Cher herself admits, she's one of pop culture's biggest survivors who hasn't always made the right moves, but she'll always be here in one form or another. Whether Cher gets panned on a Worst Dressed list, or laughed at for doing a hair infomercial, or for getting too much plastic surgery, she only does what her gut feelings guide her to do and everybody else better get out of the way!

The new millennium has Cher in the recording studio and looking into new movie roles. Her website, cher.com, is one of the most colorful on the Internet. And you'll never know where she'll pop up next.

The Lady Godiva in leather—Cher's appearance at the London premiere of *Harry Potter and the Sorcerer's Stone* in November 2001 shows that her creativity and ability to surprise will never die.

Cher debuted her first single from her new *Living Proof* album, "Song for the Lonely," at the American Music Awards on January 9, 2002. Without a doubt, she is—and will remain—Cher-rific for years to come!

Did You Know? . . .

- Chocolate is Cher's biggest downfall. "I like everything that has chocolate in it. The more chocolatey, the better," she says.

- *Sex in the City* is one of Cher's favorite television shows.

- Cher was first diagnosed with dyslexia at age thirty.

- Cher knew both poverty and wealth as a child. Her mother married men from different walks of life and she lived briefly in both Beverly Hills and a New York luxury apartment while growing up.

- In 1984, Cher received a Best Supporting Actress nomination for *Silkwood*.

- Cher admits that she always wanted to be in show business and was impressed that Sonny had music business "ins" when he met her.

- Sonny and Cher put all their own money into the making of the late sixties independent film *Chastity* and had to borrow money from their chauffeur to eat lunch.

- Cher's son, Elijah, has toured with her as a guitarist, and now he has his own rock band called Deadsy.

- Cher has always had issues with network censors, especially when she was doing the *Cher* show. She has always been a big proponent of free speech.

- It was Cher who originated the square-shaped nail look back in 1970. This nail-fashion look is still popular today.

- Cher's favorite binge foods include Entenmann's chocolate doughnuts, Reese's Pieces, barbecue-flavored potato chips, and M&Ms. Most of the time she tries to eat healthy.

- Cher's binge eating on the *Witches of Eastwick* set caused her to gain thirteen pounds in two months.

- Cher's on-line and catalog store, *Sanctuary*, sold goth and antique-style household goods, including door knockers, end tables, candle holders, and pillows.

- There is interesting "official" merchandise on Cher's website as well as a Cher Thames ring, Egyptian incense burner, and a blue, vinyl halter top.

- Cher has had entire houses decorated in the ancient Egyptian style. She is fascinated by

the fact that it was such an advanced culture for its time.

- Cher participates in many motorcycle runs for charity on her favorite black Harley.

- In 1988, Cher won the Best Actress Oscar for *Moonstruck*.

- Its been a slow process, but Cher has had some of her tattoos removed by laser surgery.

- Rumors about plastic surgery abound when it comes to Cher—from breast work to rib removal—but she only admits to having eyelid, nose, and teeth work done.

- Cher claims the saddest day of her life was when she had to deliver Sonny's eulogy. She says she didn't know she was being videotaped at the time she gave it.

Sonny & Cher star on the Hollywood Walk
of Fame.

- Cher has publicly admitted that it took her a long time to cope with the fact that her daughter, Chastity, is a lesbian.

- Cher writes in her book *The First Time* that she has an attraction to bad boys and that she once dated a married guy.

- Cher, the superstar of the seventies lived in a thirty-room mansion with five cars and six servants. Three-year-old Chas (Chastity) even had her own TV to watch *The Sonny & Cher Comedy Hour*.

- At one point in the sixties, Sonny & Cher were bigger than the Beatles in Britain.

- One of Cher's romantic liaisons before Sonny included Warren Beatty. Years later, Beatty wanted to cast Cher in the film *Bonnie & Clyde*, but Sonny refused to let her audition.

- Cher was very self-conscious about her looks as a child. Her mother and Georgeanne were blond and beautiful. I always felt short and ugly," Cher has said.

- Even after thirty-eight years in the music business, Cher claims that she still gets brutal stage fright.

- Fans on Cher's official website want Cher to rerelease *Stars*, *I'd Rather Believe in You*, *Cherished*, and *Allman and Woman: Two the Hard Way* on CD.

- Cher's first foray into serious acting was actually via her mother, Georgia Holt, who has always been friends with noted filmmaker Robert Altman.

- Cher's first off-Broadway role was in *Come Back to the 5 and Dime, Jimmy Dean, Jimmy Dean*. She admits that at first, she was intimidated by costar Sandy Dennis.

- The last episode of the *Sonny & Cher Comedy Hour* aired May 29, 1974.

- Cher has said the first record that she ever bought was "Tequila" by The Champs and that she was highly influenced by Elvis's first television appearance in 1957.

- Cher has revealed that her rocky relationship with ex-husband Gregg Allman was a "car crash ready to happen."

- Cher wore braces for five years and was embarrassed that she had to accept her Oscar while wearing them.

- She calls her black Harley her "baby fat boy."

- The *Cher* show debuted on February 16, 1975.

- Cher has been writing poetry for years. Some of it was used for songs in 1994, which later became the *not.com.mercial* CD.

- Cher was once suspended in high school for going barefoot and wearing bell-bottoms—a look that she would later make famous.

- An Arab sheik once offered Sonny two million dollars to buy Cher!

- *The Sonny & Cher Comedy Hour* debuted on CBS in August 1971.

- Cher says her son, Elijah, is "extremely sensitive and talented."

- Cher claims she didn't know how to write a check until after she divorced Sonny.

- Cher's 1965 debut album with Sonny, titled *Look at Us*, sold over one million copies when it was first released.

- In 1999, Cher was named one of *People* magazine's "Ten Worst Dressed."

- Cher met Bob Mackie back in 1968 when she guested on *The Carol Burnett Show* and Mackie was designing Burnett's gowns.

- Cher got her first tattoo right after she and Sonny separated. It was a butterfly with a flower.

- Cher's natural parents became estranged from each other due to her father's drug addiction.

- Cher is the only woman in pop-music history to have had a Top ten hit in four decades—the sixties, seventies, eighties, and nineties.

- Cher calls old-fashioned Italian guys (including Rob Camilletti) "mooks." She has always said that Rob was like "a guy from the 1940s."

- The first time Cher dyed her hair red was for the movie *Mask*. Cher admits that the colorist was a "discount guy" who did a bad job. She wound up with red-and-black, polka-dotted hair.

- In 1993, Cher went to Armenia to get in touch with her ethnic roots. She calls it, "The strangest trip I've ever taken."

- The new *Sonny & Cher Show* debuted February 1, 1976.

- Cher said Sonny was "The most unforgettable character I've ever met" after the long-standing column of that name in *Readers Digest*? She made a point of calling him that in her eulogy for him.

- Cher admits to having been at odds with David Letterman at times and has referred to him as an "a-hole".

- One of Cher's all-time favorite rock songs is "Whiter Shade of Pale" by Poco Harum.

- Audrey Hepburn became Cher's idol in 1961 after Cher saw *Breakfast at Tiffany's*. She identified strongly with Hepburn's Holly Golightly character.

- Although she loves fabulous clothes, Cher admits that she has always felt most comfortable in a pair of worn-out jeans.

- Cher used to cut Sonny's hair when they were on tour in the sixties.

- Cher has always hated being on the road, but she has dreaded playing Las Vegas the most.

- Sonny and Cher did most of their recording at Goldstar Studios in West Hollywood.

- When Sonny and Cher first appeared on the *Ed Sullivan Show*, she was embarrassed because Mr. Sullivan called her "Chur."

- Chastity's middle name, Sun, is an abbreviation for Sonny—natch!

- Chastity admits that her mother never liked that her daughter dresses in a "preppy, masculine way."

- Cher's first foray into the directing world was with the HBO movie *If These Walls Could Talk*. Cher portrayed an abortion doctor.

- Sonny and Cher recorded "Love Is Strange," "Do You Want to Dance," and "Let the Good Times Roll" as Caesar and Cleo.

- Cher admits to having a long-standing adoration of Tony Curtis. Interestingly enough, Sonny and Cher bought two Beverly Hills houses from him, including the famous St. Cloud mansion in the seventies.

- The sixties tune "Baby Don't Go" was written by Sonny on a used $85 Steinway in the couple's living room.

- Cher met Rob Camilletti on the eve of her fortieth birthday at the now-defunct New York City club Heartbreak.

- Cher refers to her Oscar as "her first golden dream man."

- By the end of 1965, Sonny & Cher had six singles in the Top Forty.

- Her first-ever nightclub act as a solo artist was at the Sahara in Las Vegas in 1978.

- Cher admits to "never knowing how to be low-key," especially when it comes to clothing.

- On their first trip to London in 1965, Sonny and Cher were thrown out of the Hilton for their "unruly" appearances.

- Cher has a climate-controlled room in her Malibu home to keep all her gowns and wigs at their ideal temperature.

- Cher rented a second Malibu home while her first house was being redecorated.

- Because Cher is dyslexic, she usually has one of her several assistants dial phone numbers for her.

- Cher's cast-offs—both home furnishings and clothing—can be purchased at auction on eBay for rather reasonable sums?

- Cher sued Sonny's estate for back alimony of one million dollars.

- It was rumored at the time of his death that Sonny and Cher were thinking of putting together a play based on their real-life story.

- Cher loves climbing into a bed made up with crispy, clean sheets.

- Cher tries to see as many new movies as her schedule allows.

- In 1965, Cher recorded "Ringo, I Love You" as Bonnie Jo Mason.

- Cher started her music career doing backing vocals on the songs "Be My Baby" by the Ronettes, "Da Do Ron Ron" by the Crystals, and the huge hit "You've Lost that Loving Feeling" by the Righteous Brothers.

- It has been rumored that the film *Chastity* was hated by Cher to the extent that she has pursued destroying as many copies as possible over the years.

- "Believe" is the biggest-selling single of Cher's career. It was number one in twenty-two countries, and sold over 6.5 million copies worldwide.

- There was actually a story line to the "If I Could Turn Back Time" video. The scenes that were cut at the last minute showed Cher in a horse-drawn carriage wearing a big cape, and also on a speedboat.

What's next for Cher?

CHAPTER FIFTEEN

Millennium Cher: Do You Believe?

The millennium proved to be quite productive for Cher. Since the turn of the century, she has kept up her schedule of television appearances, recorded a new album of songs, went on tour, and is currently finding the time to do a remake of *The Enchanted Cottage*.

Albums

Since 2000, Cher has released five albums (three were compilations) and an Internet-only collection of songs she wrote. *Living Proof*, her most recent album to date, hit the stores in late February 2002. A much-anticipated album since the success of *Believe*, Cher teamed up with *Believe* producer Mark Taylor in hopes of recreating the success of the 1998 smash album.

The first single from the album, "The Music's No Good Without You," was released November 2001 in Europe. Opening up in the European market before coming stateside is a strategy that has worked well in the past for Cher, and this time was no exception. Cher debuted a new single from *Living Proof*—"Song for the Lonely"—in the States at the 2002 American Music Awards. In addition to *Living Proof*, several Cher hits collections were released in the past couple of years including: *The Way of Love: The Cher Collection*; *Behind the Door 1964–1974*; *20th Century Masters: The Millennium Collection*, and the *Essential Collection*.

The one release that perhaps may have skipped by many of her fans and the general pub-

A blond-haired Cher. *Living Proof* was her much-anticipated album after 1998's smash hit *Believe*.

lic was her Internet-only release of not.com.mercial. This was Cher's first attempt at full-fledged songwriting. Though Cher received some mixed reviews on the collection of songs, she received the most negative feedback from church leaders regarding the track "Sisters of Mercy." In this

"When I hit fifty, I thought, 'Well, this is it. It's over.' But it isn't, you know. The rock generation just keeps going and picking up generations."

song, Cher describes some "cruel, heartless, and wicked" times she endured as a child when nuns cared for her while her mother needed to get back on her feet. Cher admits that not.com.mercial was not a polished album on purpose. It is very personal and is out there for her fans that are truly interested—and who can find it.

Television and Film Appearances

In her usual fashion, Cher managed to stay on the airwaves and on television in the new millennium. She began popping up in February 2000, with the impending release of *Living Proof*. She hit *Late Night with David Letterman*, *The Rosie O'Donnell Show*, *Larry King Live*, and *20/20*.

Cher was scheduled to perform as the special guest on Britney Spears's *Live from the MGM Grand Las Vegas* special on HBO November 18, 2001, but she had to cancel at the last second due to a prior engagement in Europe. Perhaps someday soon Cher will make it up to the pop princess, as Spears saluted Cher earlier with her pop-infused rendition of *The Beat Goes On*.

Cher also appeared in the *Will & Grace*

episode titled "Gypsies, Tramps, and Thieves," on November 16, 2000, which just happened to air during sweeps week. In the episode, the show's affable character Jack, played by actor Sean Hayes, is a huge Cher fan. In a humorous exchange, Cher and Jack have a bit of a show-down and the diva tries to prove to him that she is the real thing and not a female impersonator.

On a larger scale, Cher was a part of VH1's *Divas* which aired April 9, 2000. She joined a slew of female performers for the sold-out perfor-mance, which remains in rotation on VH1. Cher also made a personal appearance on the *I Love Lucy 50th Anniversary Special* in 2001, *TV's National Lottery Christmas Cracker* (2001), and *Royal Variety Performance 2001*.

While Cher continues to make special appearances, she recently took on a project that has been a dream of hers since the seventies. Cher purchased the film rights to *The Enchanted Cottage*, and will direct and star in the remake of this romantic drama, in which two people fall in love in a seaside cottage. It was a special year indeed for Cher as she won the Women in Film Lucy Award in 2000 sharing it with actresses Sharon Stone and Anne Heche.

New Mattel Cher Doll 2001

Cher was immortalized in plastic (again) when Mattel premiered a gorgeous new Cher doll on May 28, 2001. Her plastic persona was draped in a lavender gown designed by Bob Mackie, and the doll's "true-to-life" details include authentic face

"People are so busy looking at me that they don't feel they can be seen. I have a strange view of what's going on by watching people who think I can't see them or hear them. I'm not sure it's a fun place to be, but it's interesting and strange."

sculpting, dramatic face paint, and a mane of black hair. The plastic beauty bears a striking resemblance to its 1975 predecessor and stands eleven inches tall. However, it is also is a full inch shorter than the older Mego-made doll and does not have additional costumes or accessories. A prototype of the new Mattel Cher doll appeared on *Will & Grace*.

Through it all—four decades' worth of music, television, concerts tours, movies, and Broadway— Cher still considers herself JPC, a nickname only her closest friends and associates call her. The acronym stands for "Just Plain Cher," meaning that underneath all the glitz, she's still as real as you and me.

But how long can the beat go on? As this book went to press, it was rumored that Cher's concert tour for *Living Proof* will be the now fifty-six-year-old singer's last hooray on the road. She wants to do more movies—acting and directing in musicals. Since the success of *Moulin Rouge*, Cher believes the time is right to revive movie musicals, and who better than Cher to sing and act in a movie?

"There is no one like Cher in the entertainment business," J. Randy Taraborrelli confirms. "I don't care if she has been completely re-created by a plastic surgeon... or not... she's still magic, and I say, God bless the child. Cher's one of the few things that's been consistent in our lives during insane times and, for that alone, I think she should be greatly valued."

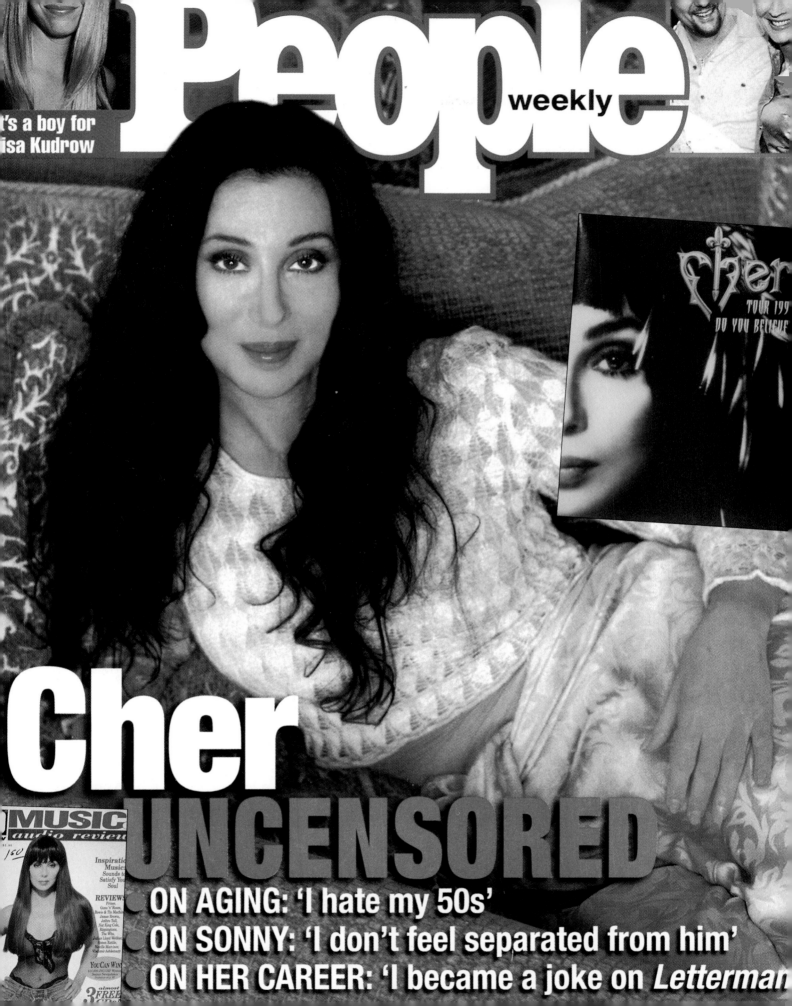

People
weekly

t's a boy for
isa Kudrow

Cher
UNCENSORED

- **ON AGING:** 'I hate my 50s'
- **ON SONNY:** 'I don't feel separated from him'
- **ON HER CAREER:** 'I became a joke on *Letterman*

MUSIC
audio review

Inspiration
Music:
Sounds to
Satisfy Your
Soul

REVIEWS
Prince,
Guns 'N' Roses,
Bowie & Tin Machine,
Jamee Brown,
Jethro Tull,
Ringo Starr,
The Who,
Julian Lloyd Webber,
Simon Rattle,
Natalie Merchant,
Vladimir Ashkenazy

YOU CAN WIN
$2,500 PRIZE! Win a
Super Sweepstakes
subscription offer $1.50

3 FREE

CHAPTER SIXTEEN

Cher: Astrologically Speaking

Birth Sign: Taurus
Birthdate: May 20, 1946
Birthplace: El Centro, California
Time of Birth: 7:25 A.M.

B orn with her sun just in Taurus, Cher's actually straddling the Taurus-Gemini cusp. She is persistent, determined, and material- istic, earthy and sensuous, as well as sta- ble, dependable, and a loyal friend and lover. Taureans are patient and thorough, which helps to explain why Cher has succeeded time and again, and despite significant odds, she simply refuses to give up.

Cher, like most Taureans, can be a bit self- indulgent at times and more than a little bit possessive. Being born so close to Gemini helps explain her smarts: she's an intellectual being whose primary urge is communication, and through communication she derives connection.

With her moon in Capricorn, Cher is most comfortable as a responsible and cautious individ- ual. This woman's successes have not been a tri- fling matter to her at all. With Capricorn's influence shining down on her, she's had the ben- efit of a hardworking, economic sensibility to help her along the way. She may have appeared to be something of a happy-go-lucky kid next to Sonny's mature wit, but you can bet that Cher played along with the full knowledge that this was her ticket to success. She also likely entered her relationship with Sonny partly on the basis of knowing he could help her get both seen and heard. With both her sun and moon in earth

signs, Cher is indeed a grounded woman, one who has a practical approach to love as well as money. Her emotions are also likely to be rather well-controlled, a key ingredient to her quest for success.

What keeps this diva rockin' the entertainment world? Only the "stars" know for sure.

145

The stars say Cher is emotionally grounded and has a positive attitude toward other people.

As her Venus is in Gemini, Cher needs to be matched intellectually where affairs of the heart are concerned, lest she get bored. She's a real thinker who gets most turned on by someone who challenges her ideas and encourages her to clarify her own thinking. While Sonny knew how to pull her strings, Cher may have wanted more from their relationship than he was able to provide.

Cher's Mercury, the planet of communication, also lies in Taurus, meaning that she'll exhibit common sense and prudent judgment along with the ability to concentrate when needed. Her Mars in Leo may be the force behind her raw star power. As Mars rules our passions—sexual and otherwise—Cher will often find herself leading the charge, exhibiting a willpower and determination that can be quite seductive.

The stars also reveal that she's an honest, down-to-earth, compassionate woman. Cher's common sense and her ability to use, enjoy, and deal effectively with the physical world are her greatest strengths. She is capable of managing practical affairs, working, and taking care of the business of day-to-day living very well. She has a strong urge to be useful and productive. For her, the bottom line is practicality: Does it work? Is it functional? Of what practical use is it? Theories and speculations mean little to her unless there is some concrete purpose, some way to use them in the real world. She is methodical and enjoys, even thrives on, a steady routine. Her first response to anything novel or experimental is caution, resistance, or skepticism. She usually makes the best of the status quo rather than venturing into the unknown or making changes that could jeopardize her security in any way.

Material security is particularly important to Cher and her sense of well-being is directly linked with financial assets or knowing she has a steady, reliable source of income. She may hold herself back or pass over opportunities simply because she cannot control or know the outcome ahead of time. Patience and persistence are her gifts, and she builds her life on a firm foundation through discipline, work, and planning.

The stars "speak" about Cher romantically. She has an affectionate, warm-hearted, congenial, and fun-loving nature, and her emotional impulses are quite strong. Forming relationships with others is important to her and she had an early desire for marriage. Her emotional life is intense and her sexuality very strong. Cher is likely to make many demands of her partner and has to guard against possessiveness, jealousy, and a tendency to force someone to love her.

Cher's attitude toward other people is very emotional and she feels a certain soul affinity with them. She has an inner need to express her feelings to others and is especially partial to groups where she can help to further their accomplishments.

In love, Cher is more interested in a person's sense of humor and intelligence than in his or her physique. She becomes restless and bored with someone who never asks questions, who never changes or surprises her. Talking, sharing ideas, going places together, and learning new things

The stars reveal that the Dark Lady's most outstanding qualities are that she is a steadfast and patient soul, capable of tremendous devotion, dedication, endurance, and constancy.

together is very important to her happiness. She needs lots of social stimulation, is something of a flirt, and likes to have many friends of both sexes. A possessive, jealous partner is very stifling for her. She often hides her affection, or finds her feelings difficult to express to the person she loves. Being openly affectionate and trusting often doesn't seem safe to her.

Cher may feel her love won't be appreciated or reciprocated. She may get involved in secret love affairs or fall in love with a person who is quite unavailable to her. Love and sacrifice often seem to go hand in hand for her—having to give something up to be with the one she loves, or having to relinquish some person or some aspect of an important love relationship. Cher tends to suppress her feelings and approach other people with great reserve. She may feel lonesome, but unable to bridge the gap between herself and others. But once she enters a relationship, she will be faithful and steady in her feelings for her partner.

The stars show she has quirky tendencies and craves excitement. Cher tends to have strange idiosyncrasies and domestic habits, and she may feel that she doesn't fit in with "normal" people. These could be endearing eccentricities or truly outlandish behavior and tastes.

Establishing a steady routine and rhythm in

her life would be very beneficial to Cher, but may not be easily achieved. Ideally, she can create a unique lifestyle that affords her a lot of personal space, freedom, and flexibility to follow her somewhat erratic rhythms, while at the same time providing some order and consistency. There also is a current of emotional discontent or restlessness within her, which may be reflected in unstable personal relationships of the on-again/off-again variety. Whether she realizes it consciously or not, she craves change and excitement.

The stars reveal challenges and difficulties in Cher's everyday life. Cher fears becoming emotionally dependent upon others and may distance herself or deny her needs for closeness and intimacy so that she won't be vulnerable to rejection or abandonment. On the other hand, she may cling excessively or need constant reassurance from loved ones and family. Developing a deep, inner sense of security, as well as the ability to give and receive nurturing are important tasks for her. Cher has a mature, disciplined, serious attitude toward life which colors everything she does. Caution and realism are her virtues, though she limits herself at times by being too careful, shy, or fearful, and not believing in herself enough or being assertive when necessary. Others may find her difficult to get to know intimately, as she tends to distance herself from them or to put forth a rather stern, "adult" face to the world.

Cher has an inner conflict between idealism, hope, and faith in the future versus doubt and oppression by limitations and practical realities. Cher needs to develop discipline and patience in order to achieve her aspirations. She will grow by learning to accept frustration and to persevere in spite of obstacles.

The stars reveal the Dark Lady's very best qualities: a steadfast and patient soul, capable of tremendous devotion, dedication, endurance, and constancy. The ability to follow through and stick with things is one of her greatest assets. Once her course is set, she pursues it tenaciously until it is completed, stubbornly resisting any attempts to sway her from her purpose.

CHAPTER SEVENTEEN

Collecting Cher

Cher's incredible career has spanned over four decades and keeps getting stronger as Cher is introduced to a new generation of fans. Collecting Cher in the new millennium has never been so satisfying for fans of all ages—not to mention profitable.

There are over seventy different studio and compilation CDs, over sixty CD singles, various boxed CD sets, hundreds of promotional items, and official merchandise to collect for Cher and Sonny & Cher. But the latest craze in Cher collecting is purchasing her personally owned clothes (as briefly mentioned in Chapter Six). You can own an item of Cher apparel by logging on to eBay.com and searching for the popular sellers' names Starwares or Cherwares, or visit www.starwares.com.

Starwares Collectibles is located in Agoura, California. Marcia Tysseling, the owner and a longtime Cher fan, has literally hundreds of personal items that come directly from the diva herself and all are reasonably priced. Besides Cher's cast-off clothing, various other personal items are available including jewelry, accessories, sterling teapots, paintings, and more. "Most of Cher's items are fairly current," Tysseling said. "Granted, she's known for her own style, which could make it difficult to tell. But most clothing items that come my way are in excellent condition and are newer styles. Cher's jewelry and small furnishings do very well, too, as they serve as conversation pieces and as things that can be used. Our personal favorite is when we get a necklace or piece of jewelry that Cher has made herself. That's always special." A part of the profits goes to Children's Craniofacial Association and the buyer receives a C.O.A. (certificate of authenticity).

Starwares originally started selling movie props and clothing and eventually obtained items from *Mermaids* in 1990. It wasn't long before they were consigning all of Cher's personal cast-offs and belongings. Tysseling first met Cher in 1989 through the star's former manager, Bill Sammeth, and recalled, "Cher and I both lived in the same, small community in Malibu. I was literally at one end of the street and she was on the other. Most of the time, Deb Paull or Jennifer Ruiz (her assistants) call me when they are ready for me to pick

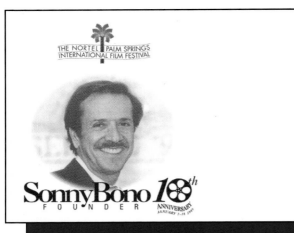

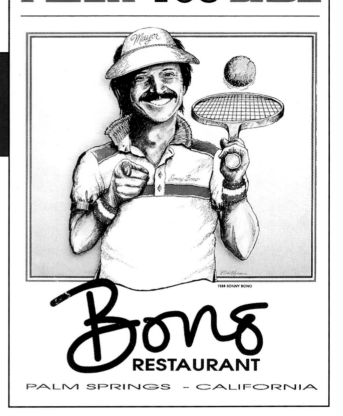

Two rare Sonny Bono paper items: Bono's Palm Springs, California, restaurant postcard and the 1999 10th Anniversary Palm Springs Film Festival commemorative.

things up. The Cher items are typically bagged, boxed, and ready to go. . . ."

Another popular eBay seller of Cher memorabilia is Chuck Swift, eBay name SonCher98. Swift has been selling Sonny and Cher pieces on-line since 1998, when he came into legal possession of Sonny's personal belongings. "I own the rights and these items." Swift said. "All items we have in stock come with 'C.O.A.' and guaranteed provenance as having come from Sonny's personal items while here in Palm Springs. We are one of the West Coast's largest collections of 'authentic' Sonny & Cher memorabilia. Currently we have over five hundred rare and one-of-a-kind items. Our customers are very happy with what we sell them. We have the glowing feedback from eBay to prove it!"

Some of Swift's more popular Sonny Bono and Cher items have included Sonny's tuxedo suits, stage pants, a *Comedy Hour* show jacket, watches, sunglasses, costume jewelry, and outfits worn by Cher from the show, and personal Bono family photos and letters.

Celebrity clothing and personal item collecting through Internet auctions that take place on eBay, Yahoo, and Amazon have become popular over the past few years. The best advice Swift can offer to a seasoned Cher memorabilia collector

who knows the value of vinyl albums, forty-five singles, eight tracks, promotional photos, and so on, but has no clue as to how to find the significance of "worn by Cher" items, is to not to feel pressured to own everything once worn or used by Cher. It's more important to collect pieces that can be authenticated and come with a money-back guarantee. "The smartest advice is to start simply," says Swift, "and be very wary of a lot of things. Be very careful of the authentication of any item. Ask if it's guaranteed to be an authentic item. Have that seller send a verifiable copy of the C.O.A. prior to the end of the auction."

Remember the original bobcat vests? Swift sold the only two Sonny had left in a private auc-

Top Five Wish List of Cher Collectibles Fans Want to Own

In the survey for the book, dozens of serious collecting fans were asked to name the top-five items of Cher's they would like to own. Here they are:

1. A Bob Mackie gown.
2. Original pair of Sonny or Cher's bell-bottom pants from the sixties.
3. The piano on which Sonny wrote "Baby Don't Go" and "I Got You Babe."
4. One of Cher's wigs.
5. A stage prop, wardrobe piece, or costume jewelry from the *Sonny & Cher Comedy Hour*.

tion at over a thousand dollars each. Only a serious collector would understand the true value of a higher-end item like the fur vests or tuxedo suits and be in the position to afford such extravagance. If you plan on collecting Cher's clothing, remember in most cases it is going to be a higher-end item.

Wondering about the authenticity of the autographed pic of Cher you just paid forty-five dollars for on-line? Ask to see a C.O.A. from the seller. Swift is often asked to authenticate autographed photos of Cher and Sonny, too, and you'd be surprised at how many are fakes. "It's true," he said. "Back in the early sixties through the seventies, Cher spent a lot of time coming up with that key signature and the true fans know what that is. . . . She wanted to have a very unique signature and she has really never deviated from that."

Collecting Cher and or Sonny & Cher should be a jovial journey. If you can't buy something you want the first time around on-line you will most likely have a second chance to find it. Simply enjoy the experience. Who knows, you might make some new friends along the way and trade items from your collections.

Sonny & Cher Dolls, Toys, and Other Memorabilia

Variety shows were very popular during the 1970s. Many television studios felt that all they needed was a big-name star, a few good jokes, a dash of flash, and some bubbly music to create a variety series for the viewing audience. Unfortunately, most of these programs vanished from the airwaves almost as quickly as they appeared. Ever heard of *The New Bill Cosby Show*, *The Brady Bunch Hour*, *The Don Knotts Show*, or *The Glenn Campbell Goodtime Hour*? From the slew of short-lived flops rose a few notable standouts that lasted more than one season. *Donny & Marie* and *The Flip Wilson Show* among them. *The Flip Wilson Show* even shot to the number-two spot of the Nielsen Ratings during its first year.

Not as commercially successful, but probably the most-remembered variety series of the seventies, was *The Sonny & Cher Comedy Hour*. Introduced as a trial run in the summer of 1971, Sonny

A selection of Sonny & Cher dolls.

HALF-BREED

Music by
AL CAPPS

ANG
ME)

BANG
(OT ME)

SONNY BONO

.7

HALF-BREED

Lyrics by MARY DEAN
Music by AL CAPPS
As Recorded by CHÉR
on MCA Records

Produced by
Snuff Garrett

BLUE MONDAY MU

1.50

325

Bang Bang   that aw

ground_Bang Bang   that aw

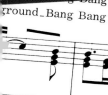

A *Sonny & Cher Comedy Hour* admission ticket.

and Cher found a permanent home on the CBS network's midseason schedule. It wasn't an instant hit, but somehow the show managed to sneak into the number-eight spot when no one was looking.

Salvatore Bono and Cherilyn LaPierre were the main characters of an unlikely success story. They had met in the mid-sixties while Sonny was a struggling songwriter/musician and Cher an aspiring actress and singer. It wasn't long before they were married and teamed up to spend almost a decade performing in clubs and auditoriums. Considered "rock freaks" by other musicians and much of the public, the Bonos sported unconventional bangs and fur vests. They didn't seem to fit in, but Sonny was determined that their talent would prevail. What he didn't know was that their tours allowed them to hone their greatest future asset—the interplay between husband and wife on stage.

Ford 1966 Sonny & Cher trading card.

Sonny's perseverance eventually led to the idea that their routine would be great material for a comedy show on television. Their hit single "I Got You Babe" gave them the leverage they needed to land the singing, dancing, and comedy show

The Sonny & Cher Comedy Hour from 1971 to 1974. The recurring comedy sketches included Cher's "Vamp" segments in which she portrayed notorious women in history; "Sonny's Pizza" segment featuring Sonny as the dumb owner of a pizza parlor and Cher as waitress Rosa; "Dirty Linen" segments with Cher as "Laverne," sharing her views on men with a friend at the Laundromat; and headline news spoofs.

By May of 1974, the *The Sonny & Cher Comedy Hour* was at its peak of popularity and reached its highest spot in the ratings. The Bono's marriage wasn't quite as successful. Their union dissolved a few months before the end of the third season, and to the disappointment of viewers across the country, their television show met an equally abrupt demise. Citing that they could no longer work together, they both made an attempt to continue alone. Within months, *The Sonny Comedy Revue* premiered on NBC, and Cher was televised by CBS. It was soon obvious that the chemistry they had together didn't emerge on their own. Both series were canceled within the first year on the air.

Sonny had always been the one to forge new

Rare Sonny & Cher concert programs.

ventures for the duo in the past, but in 1976 Cher asked Sonny to reunite their television partnership for *The Sonny & Cher Show*. Even though their private lives were headed in different directions, they revived their comedy and singing personas to try and recapture the magic. Sonny and Cher weren't able to recover their original variety show audience, and the reunion ended in little over a year.

I Got Toys Babe

Anticipating another hit show, the Mego Company designed a line of Sonny and Cher dolls and accessories in 1976. Both dolls were 12¼-inch replicas, fully jointed, and closely resembled the stars. Sonny came in one version. He was dressed in blue jeans, white shirt, and black shoes, and was packaged in a window-display box. Cher, on the other hand, was issued in a few variations. To match the Sonny doll, one was created with a dark skin tone, rooted eyelashes, and long, silky black hair. Wearing a pink dress, she, too, was packaged in a window-display box. Both can be found for between seventy-five to one hundred dollars each.

Another Cher doll by Mego was packaged in a red window-display box with a photo of Cher appearing on the box front. The doll body was molded differently. The doll head was the same,

Four popular Sonny & Cher toys from 1976: Cher's Sing-Along Phono, Cher Makeup Center, Sonny & Cher Hers & His Customizing Car Kit, and the Cher Travel Trunk.

Growing Hair Cher in original packaging.

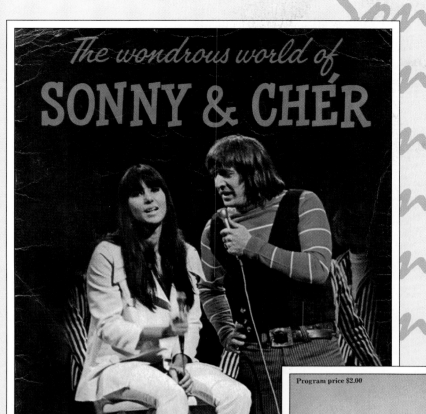

The wondrous world of **SONNY & CHÉR**

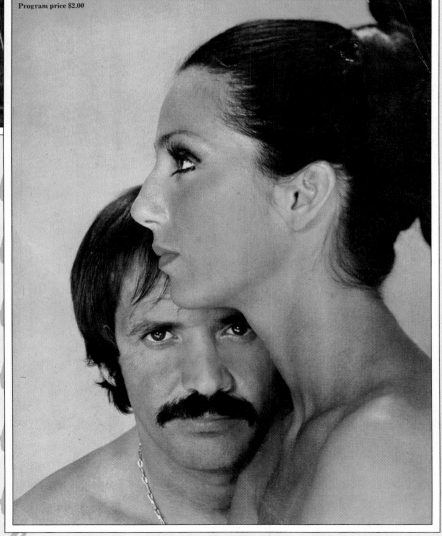

Program price $2.00

but the body was nonarticulated and made out of hollow plastic. This same doll was also packaged in a clear plastic bag. The red-boxed doll is valued at seventy-five dollars, while the bagged version is worth about fifty dollars. The most deluxe edition of the Cher doll was the Growing Hair Cher, which came in three different box designs. Cher's long, black mane could become even longer by pulling the thick strands out from the back of her head. Don't worry, they were easily tucked back in place by pulling the ring from her back. Expect to pay nearly double over the standard-issue doll to add this one to your collection.

The same fashion designer that created Cher's extravagant gowns for *The Sonny & Cher Comedy Hour* was enlisted to design small-scale versions for the doll. Bob Mackie fashions by Mego were equally extravagant, but may be considered gaudy by today's standards. The names of the ensembles

Sonny and Cher dolls.

give insight as to what was packaged in each window-display box and blister card. Cher outfits can be found on blue cards, green, purple, and black boxes.

There were over thirty designs with names like Electric Feathers, Indian Squaw, Laverne, Fortune Teller, Pink Fluff, and Pink Panther. The carded versions can be found for thirty to fifty dollars each, while some of the box styles can go for seventy-five dollars and up. Bob Mackie obviously enjoyed creating Cher fashions more than those for Sonny. Only six Sonny versions were made, including Private Eye, Space Prince, Buckskin, Hoedown, Gypsy King, and White Tux. They are valued between twenty-five and thirty-five dollars.

Besides doll outfits, Mego produced other doll accessories. Cher's dressing room was available as a playset for the dolls. The set was designed to fold open into a backstage dressing room. It included a couch, coffee table, dressing table, and hangers for a wardrobe closet. Magic-mirror cards were included to give the illusion that Cher could see her reflection while wearing one of her designer gowns. New magic-mirror cards were available with some of the boxed outfits sold separately. Cher's dressing room is valued at seventy-five to one hundred dollars when found in the original box. The Cher Travel Trunk was designed to store the dozens of Bob Mackie fashions. Housed in a red box, the trunk exterior featured travel stickers to showcase the many imaginary exotic locations the Cher doll had visited such as Spain, the Caribbean, and Mexico. Only six hangers were included— minimal compared to the number of outfits that could be purchased. The trunk also featured an accessories drawer. This is one of the most difficult Cher accessories to find, resulting in a 125 to 150 dollar price tag.

The largest Mego collectible in size is the Sonny & Cher's Theater in the Round. The square box was only a few inches deep, but over 2½ feet wide. Inside were pieces that assembled into a stage with three revolving rooms. A dressing room, stage, and backstage included a vanity with chair, piano, bench, microphone, stool, spotlights, television camera, and backdrops.

Due to the couple's untimely separation during the production of this item, two packaging variations can be found. The front label that originally pictured both Sonny and Cher was simply

Cher's autograph from the 1980s.

replaced with one displaying only Cher. Cher's Theatre in the Round, as well as Sonny and Cher's Theater, are both valued between 175 to 200 dollars. Perhaps the most rare doll accessory was Mego's Sonny and Cher Chevy Roadster. The red sport vehicle seemed a bit under scale in size, as the two dolls would share little space while touring around in this snug, plastic jalopy. Packaged in a matching red box with a photo of the dolls in the car, it is valued at about 200 dollars.

And the Toys Go On

As Sonny and Cher memorabilia was quickly filling store aisles in 1976, it became evident that everything was coming from the Mego Corporation. In addition to dolls and accessories, there was a handful of other items Mego made to dazzle fans. Cher's head and bust were transformed into a lifelike plastic replica for two different styling centers. One, labeled as a Cher Makeup Center, included a variety of makeup, hair brushes and ribbons, eye lashes, and vinyl signature bag. Another set came with similar contents and was packaged as a Growing Hair Styling Center. This head set included extra locks of hair that could be pulled from the back and put back in place with the pull of a string—much like that of the Growing Hair Cher doll. Each boxed styling center is valued at seventy-five to one hundred dollars.

Young girls could also accessorize themselves with Cher Jewelry. More of a toy then actual gems, these eccentric sets include pieces such as a large, wooden, logo necklace, hoop earrings, and beaded wristband. Each set was packaged on a 9 × 11½-inch blister card containing a unique illustration of the superstar. A tote bag featuring Cher's logo was also available—possibly to hold all the valuable jewelry sets.

In 1977, Mego introduced their last item in this extraordinary line of memorabilia. Cher's Sing-Along Phono was packaged with a photograph of Cher sporting her newly trimmed and curled hairdo on the box front. Other sides of the box picture previous Cher Mego products. The record player includes a working microphone, amplifier, and adapter and an embossed Cher logo on the lid. The price of this musical number will surpass any other Sonny or Cher Mego products.

For older fans beyond doll play, there were several Sonny and Cher paper commodities available. The famous pop duo graced the cover of numerous magazines during their heyday, while Cher took center stage as the subject of a few books. For under a dollar, *TV & Movie Screen*, *Rona Barrett's Hollywood*, and *Photo Screen* were quick to reveal the couple's private lives, rare photos, and some behind-the-scenes gossip. Today, these informative publications can be acquired

Superstar of the Seventies: Cher! book.

for about twenty-five dollars each. Paperback books of Cher bring in about the same value and include titles such as *Superstar of the Seventies: CHER!*, *Cher*, and *Simply Cher*. If owning all the toys, magazines, and books still leaves a void in your collection, there is an abundance of music-related paraphernalia to collect.

Because the pair started their recording career in the mid-sixties, there are many albums, singles, tour books, and music sheets to uncover. With words and music by Sonny himself, "The Beat Goes On" is one of the most coveted of all their music sheets. Recorded in 1967, this Top ten hit became the theme to their television show. The youthful couple is pictured on the 9 × 12-inch cover, which holds a value of about thirty dollars. From the vinyl collection, one of the more obscure items to find is a tiny, 4-inch flexi-disc given out by Ford Motor Company. The record came sealed in a red, paper envelope that sported an early photo of Sonny & Cher and included their number-one hit "I Got You Babe" and "The Beat Goes On." Today, this mini-disc is valued at forty dollars.

A selection of Cher and Sonny & Cher CDs.

Two Sonny & Cher
forty-five singles:
"Little Man" Italian
picture sleeve and
"Baby Don't Go."

The "I Got You Babe" Check List

- 12¼″ Cher Doll, Mego, 1976 (deluxe box version).
- 12¼″ Cher Doll, Mego, 1976 (budget box version).
- 12¼″ Cher Doll, Mego, 1976 (bag version).
- 12¼″ Cher Doll Outfits, Mego, 1976 (boxed).
- 12¼″ Cher Doll Outfits, Mego, 1976 (carded).
- 12¼″ Growing Hair Cher Doll, Mego, 1976.
- 12¼″ Sonny Doll, Mego, 1976.
- 12¼″ Sonny Doll Outfits, Mego, 1976 (boxed).
- Book, *Simply Cher*, EMC Corporation, 1975.
- Calendar, MCA, 1972.
- Cher Jewelry, Mego, 1976.
- Cher Tote Bag, Mego, 1976.
- Cher Travel Trunk, Mego, 1976.
- Cher's Dressing Room Playset, Mego, 1976.
- Cher's Makeup Center, Mego, 1976.
- Cher's Growing Hair Styling Center, Mego, 1976.
- Cher's Sing-Along Phono, Mego, 1977.
- Dress Patterns (for 12¼″ doll).
- Hip-Pocket Record, "I Got You Babe," Philco, 1973.
- Paperback book, *Superstar of the Seventies: CHER!*, Ballantine Books, 1975.
- Posters (various).
- Records—forty-fives and LPs (various).
- Sheet music (various).
- Sonny and Cher's Theatre in the Round, Mego (also just Cher's Theater).
- Sonny and Cher's Roadster, Mego (for 12¼″ dolls).
- Sonny and Cher's Mustang Model Kit.
- School Folders (Cher's image on front).
- Tour books and programs.

—Bill Morgan

Hip-Pocket Record, "I Got You Babe" and "The Beat Goes On."

A Cher Friends fan club folder, circa 1977.

Sonny and Cher

Dear Friends:

When we first started recording we were receiving a
nominal amount of mail from all our friends. CHER and
I would set a day aside every week to answer all the mail
ourselves. But as time went on the mail increased con-
siderably and we got much busier, which presented a problem
because we were no longer able to answer our mail personally.

Then we hired a secretary to attend to it and assign Fan
Clubs throughout the country. But even this didn't work
out because the mail continued to increase. To make a
long story short, the mail got heavier and we got busier,
which brings us up to right now.

Although it is very flattering that so many people care
enough about us to write to us in such quantity, I am sure
you can now understand that it is impossible for us to
answer your letters personally. To compensate for this,
and to be as fair as possible, here's what we've decided to
do:

Anyone who wishes to write us, or be a Fan, should write to
the address below. 'Though not personally, all mail will
be answered along with an autographed picture, a membership
card if you desire, and an occassional form letter letting
you know what's going on as far as we're concerned, since
this seems to be the main request of 90% of our mail. There
will be no charge -- if you include return postage we will
take care of everything else.

Thank you for your letters and thoughtfulness.

Love,

Sonny

Cher

SONNY & CHER

Fan Mail Address: 8560 Sunset Boulevard, Los Angeles, Calif. 90069

An original 1965 fan club letter written by Sonny & Cher.

AMI SPECIALS

WINTER 2000

cher

EXPOSED

Her life in pictures

HER SIZZLING LOVE LIFE

REAL REASON SHE DIVORCED SONNY

HER FABULOUS FASHIONS

HER AMAZING CAREER

CHAPTER EIGHTEEN

The Cher Society

Cher has had so many devoted fans over the past four decades. There are literally thousands who quiver at the mention of her single-word name. At the time of writing this book, a man from Houston, Texas, was seriously thinking of emptying his 401(k) retirement savings just to have the privilege of hiring the legendary performer for his fortieth birthday party. "Is he a gay guy?" a surprised Cher responded when a reporter asked why she inspires such a strong allegiance of followers. "Gay fans are with you no matter what," she explained. "They kind of stick with you whether you're down or up, if you're happy or have a nervous breakdown." It's not just gay fans, Cher, but fans of all ages and from all walks of life.

A quick glance of Cher fan websites on the Internet revealed over four-hundred, and many are international website tributes—some from as far away as Australia, Singapore, and Germany. "If you've been around as long as I've been around," Cher noted, "people grow up and associate good times with you. They either wish you well, or they don't care one way or another."

An informal survey of Cher (and Sonny Bono) fans conducted for this book via the Internet and the 2000 Cher Convention revealed that the Dark Lady's appeal is not only unique, but extraordinary. Perhaps what fans admire most about Cher, besides her music and movies, is her refreshing honesty and straightforwardness. Despite repeated derision by the press media, she has never retreated, yielded, or even winced. There are times she regrets her candor, saying she naïvely opened up her personal life to close examination, but she admits that she feels inept eluding or deceiving reporters. Facing adversity and media criticism since the sixties, Cher says: "You never get used to it. You cry and cry and cry until you're finished. Just because you keep going doesn't mean you're not devastated. You just don't show it."

What Are Fans Saying?

Rose DelGardo from New Rochelle, New York, responded: "Cher is one of a kind. She is loving, caring, and giving to the causes that she believes in and she is not afraid to tell people what she thinks of them. She holds nothing back. She is cool and down to earth and that's what we love about her. She is for real. There is nothing phony about her. Cher is a big part of my life and she has influenced me in a positive way because she is so open and straightforward and not afraid to speak her mind. It is so great that there are so many people that feel like I do about Cher. She is so loved by so many and does so much for the unfortunate."

"I have been a loyal fan since 1965," Josie Caruso Sethi writes. "I have seen Sonny and Cher ten times in concert since 1967 and have met them on three separate occasions. I have a collection that spans nearly four decades. I can still remember the debut of "The Beat Goes On" on the radio and seeing them in concert. My dad had a Super 8

169

"If you've been around as long as I've been around, people grow up and associate good times with you."

170

camera in 1967 and filmed the most incredible concert footage of Sonny and Cher's live performances and colorful costumes at the Ohio State Fair. In the footage from one concert, there was this huge bruise on Cher's upper thigh. More importantly, the camera captured the intense love between a very happily married couple. For me and most fans like me, this was Sonny and Cher at the purest time of their marriage and career. I will never forget how love radiated that day from the stage."

————————————————

Over the past four decades, Cher has attained a wide circle of fans ranging from as young as age five to as old as eighty-five. With each new project, whether it's recording an album, making a film, or going on a concert tour, Cher always seems to win over new converts—and her longtime legion of faithful followers remain forever connected to her, perhaps stronger now than ever before.

If you were to create a formula for success, Cher's career would make an outstanding model. From music and film to concert performances and television appearances and her hands-on involvement with the Children's Craniofacial Association, this multifaceted entertainer has been and will always be one of the chosen few from a small and elite group of timeless icons. Her many splendored songs will be referenced and called to mind for years to come, even as songs from lesser artists fade away. Her amazing and unselfish desire to see the end of child and adult suffering from facial deformities has set a high example for others to follow.

One can see that this truly remarkable woman and a multifaceted entertainer who deserves every fan she has earned. There's no doubt that the

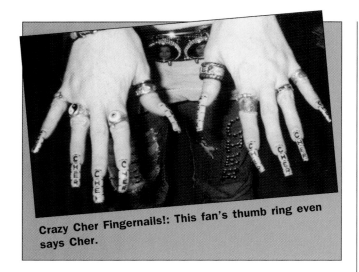
Crazy Cher Fingernails!: This fan's thumb ring even says Cher.

faithful will stick with Cher through every stage of her fascinating and enduring career. There seems to be a true sense that thousands really identify with her and easily relate to the songs she sings and the characters she portrays in movies. "I have great respect for her ability of giving people hope again through her music," said Lisa Womack from Dallas, Texas. "Cher is a true survivor and inspiration. Throughout Cher's career, she has suffered but kept fighting her own demons and life's evils and did not give up on life or humanity. She has defied the odds of stardom and is doing more now then ever for herself and for others. She is such an inspiration to us all."

━ ━ ━ ━ ━ ━ ━ ━ ━ ━ ━ ━

Brad Wright from Calgary, Alberta, Canada, has always felt a connection to Cher's music and in-your-face attitude about life. "Much like Cher, I have always felt different than people around me and that I didn't belong," he said. "This is strange because many of the Cher fans that I have met over the years have shared the same feelings. Cher's music has gotten me through many tough times. For example, the song "Love and Pain" from *Take Me Home* got me through my mom's death. I was always able to escape into Cher's music and resurface refreshed."

━ ━ ━ ━ ━ ━ ━ ━ ━ ━ ━ ━

Stacey Johnson from Buffalo, New York, wrote: "I saw the *Sonny & Cher Comedy Hour* on television when I was nine years old. The first time I saw

Cher being presented with the key to the city in Sydney, Australia, 1990.

Meeting fans.

Cher I thought she was the most beautiful woman in the world. I kept watching her show, but I had to watch it in secret. My parents thought Cher was not a good role model for young girls. I remember being very upset because I really loved the show. Growing up I always felt ugly and had to dress in these old hand-me-down clothes. But when I looked at Cher, I somehow had hope that I could grow up and make something of my life. Cher made me see that I was beautiful. I am a nurse now, and collecting anything-Cher is my hobby."

John Hostetler from Ohio has been a lifelong Cher fan and said he was immediately taken by her stunning dark looks and her barely there Bob Mackie gowns. "Cher to me—a ten-year-old boy at the time—was like no other performer I had ever seen before on television. I loved her looks, her clothes, and her singing voice—the sexy way she would sing those solo torch songs."

It's not just the old faithful that admire Cher and the music she makes. The under-twenty crowd revere her as well. Cyrinda Thomas is fourteen years old and a second generation fan who accompanies her mom, Joyce, to Cher's concerts. "I love Cher so much," she said. "I liked her since 1996. She is so cool and puts on the best concert ever! My mom took me to see the *Believe* tour and I was just so mesmerized. I wasn't born when 'Half Breed' and 'Dark Lady' were popular in the seventies, but I love to see Cher sing them live. It's such a thrilling experience."

There is no doubt that Cher will remain one of the most beloved stars of the twenty-first century. This fan survey embodied many significant aspects of the legendary entertainer's lure, beginning with a question on how one became a fan in the first place. The number-one response was the inevitable, her music, followed closely by her

(text continued on page 180)

Cher Through the Artists' Eye

On canvas in art galleries, Cher's face and figure have been the inspiration for many interpretations. Her exotic features, especially her Native American looks—the famous cheekbones and signature, long black hair—and the famous Mackie outfits, have caused many artists, amatuer and professional alike to want to depict Cher's beauty on canvas. Dozens of talented fans sent in wonderful submissions for this book, and we're just sorry we couldn't print them all. Here are some of the more interesting artists' renditions of Cher.

By Pam Roberts

Through her career's highs and lows, there's no doubt that Cher's fans truly love her for life.

By Pam Roberts '00.

CHÉR

By Pam Roberts

concert performances and film roles. Cher herself will tell you that she doesn't understand why people love and revere her so much, but at the same time, she is grateful for all the attention.

As a performer, Cher is no less than the consummate showwoman giving her all to her fans. It's no surprise that many Cher fans have seen her perform live in concert numerous times. In fact, some have even seen her dozens of times comparing and sharing musical memories from the 1989 *Heart of Stone* tour at the Mirage in Las Vegas, where Cher wore several wild outfits, and her 1999–2000 *Believe* world tour, for which Cher would still pull out some of her most glitzy stage outfits.

Rick DeSilva from Honolulu, Hawaii, who has been a fan for over thirty years, explained: "People in general (mainly the press) should get over this kick of associating Cher exclusively with gays. When she first started, her primary audience for years were mainly straight. It is Chastity who's gay, not Cher. She's just lucky enough to appeal to both groups."

Pam Roberts from Cedar Rapids, Iowa, finds Cher fans to be like a family and has made many friendships over the years. "We fans have a common bond already," she noted. "One that runs very

Cher's biggest supporters of course include her children, Chastity and Elijah, as seen in 1981.

deep. It is almost surreal. At the first Cher Convention two years ago, everyone knew everyone else. Either by sight or trading in the mail or by e-mail. We all bonded instantly. Where else in the world can a girl find herself at a dinner table seated next to a Cher impersonator while everyone joins in for an off-key rendition of 'Just This One Time'? Most people who don't know Cher don't have a clue what that song is. But we all did. And that's the bond."

Jody Cantwell, an organizer for the national Cher Convention added: "I became a fan when I heard 'The Beat Goes' On on AM radio in 1967. Then I fell in love with Cher when the *Sonny & Cher Comedy Hour* debuted. 'Just This One Time' from the *Stars* album is one of my all-time favorite Cher songs. I like it because she is asking to be able to have a chance to prove herself after leaving Sonny."

Fans from around the world sing Cher's praises through the Internet, the medium through which the Cher Convention was born. "Through the convention, Cher fans meet semiannually and raise money for the Children's Craniofacial Association," Cantwell said. "These fans are really great. They have a blast on the Net and then meet in person at the Cher Convention. We can't help but love Cher. She is such a cool person."

When asked to explain what makes Cher incomparable in the eyes of over four generations of followers, a variety of responses were generated—the biggest reason being that she is a true entertainment legend who appeals to all ages. Second to this, fans revere Cher's natural singing and acting skills, claiming that perhaps in their eyes no one even comes close to her caliber (except perhaps Barbara Streisand). One respondent wrote: "There is nobody better than Cher when it comes to performing. There is no question that Cher is extremely talented, whether it's singing, perform-

With sister, Georgeanne, in 1990.

ing live, or acting in a film. Cher always dazzles. She has done it all. Her approach to life is fascinating, too."

Survey respondents also sensed that Cher possesses qualities that they could possibly look for in a special friend: honesty, loyalty, generosity, and genuine concern for one's fellow man. When describing what makes Cher unique to so many, respondents stressed how she has changed their lives on a deeply personal level. "I was about thirteen years old, and suffering a major bout of depression," says Erika DeCiutiis of Warwick, Rhode Island. "But I didn't know that that's what it was. I only knew how horrible I felt. I sincerely wanted to take my own life. Then my dad got me tickets to see Cher in concert. If I went through with taking my own life, I'd miss the concert. In the days leading up to the show, a pattern emerged. One that would save my life. I watched Cher on television, listened to every album I could find. I absorbed it all. It took my mind off of things, made me realize that I could, in fact, be a happy person. I mostly have Cher and her work to thank for that."

One survey respondent who only referred to herself as a "Mrs. Flax" (the name of Cher's character in *Mermaids*) was able to recall the exact moment she became a true fan. "There's something about Cher that has always touched me so deeply. I attended a Sonny & Cher concert in 1977 and saw them sing their hits from the sixties. The audience went wild. Then later Cher came out in this absolutely stunning red, Indian-headdress outfit. I had never seen anything like that before. I have been a loyal fan from that moment on."

This survey was conducted one month prior to the release of *Living Proof*, Cher's latest album and the highly anticipated studio follow-up to 1998's *Believe*. Introductory tracks "(This Is) A Song for the Lonely," "The Music's No Good Without You," and "Different Kind of Love Song" were being played on the radio in different parts of Europe as well as on the Internet. In various Cher on-line newsgroups, fans were favoring "(This Is) A Song For the Lonely" as Cher's next, big, hit single. "It's the exact kind of song one would expect from Cher," offered Ronald Brunson from Denver, Colorado. "This is simply one of her very best and ranks up there with 'I Found Someone,' 'If I Could Turn Back Time,' and 'Believe.'" The overall consensus of *Living Proof* from fans is that they think it is her best work ever, right up there with *Heart of Stone* and *Believe*.

The survey asked fans what their all-time favorite Cher song is. The top three included "Gypsies, Tramps, and Thieves," "If I Could Turn Back Time," and "Believe." Other favorites included "Half Breed," "The Way of Love," "I Found Someone," "We All Sleep Alone," and "Heart of Stone." Many respondents thought their favorite Sonny & Cher songs should be included: Hands down, "I Got You Babe" was the number-one choice, followed by "Baby Don't Go." It's Hard to believe, but "The Beat Goes On" was not mentioned once.

What was the favorite Sonny & Cher album? Most fans in their late forties to mid-fifties cited 1965 debut album *Look at Us* or the 1967 *In Case You're in Love* album. Fans in their early to mid-forties chose the 1972 *All I Ever Need Is You* album.

For solo Cher—aside from Top Forty choice—favorite album cuts "Just This One Time" and "Geronimo's Cadillac" from the 1975 *Stars* album and the 1987 version of "Bang Bang" were the top-three choices, while "Carousel Man" and "I Saw a Man and He Danced with His Wife" came in as close seconds.

The survey also asked respondents to name their three favorite Cher albums. The best-selling 1998 *Believe* came in first place, followed by the 1975 *Stars* and the 1989 *Heart of Stone*. The 1987 self-titled *Cher*, 1973's *Half Breed*, *Bittersweet White Light*, and the 1971 self-titled *Cher* earned several mentions, as did 1969's *3614 Jackson Highway*. Many respondents twenty-five and under still chose *Believe* as their favorite album.

The survey also asked fans from around the world to name their favorite Cher decade. The present-day Cher took in a majority of the votes.

Of course, this survey wouldn't be complete without asking fans what their least-favorite Cher song and album are. That was an unanimous choice: the 1979 offering, *Prisoner*, was the least-loved album and the least-favorite song was "Rudy" from the 1982 *I Paralyze* album.

The survey also asked participants to name their favorite and least-favorite Cher movie. It was also nearly unanimous: *Moonstruck* came in first and *Mask* second, followed by *Mermaids* and *Tea With Mussolini*. The least-favorite Cher film was *Faithful*. Next to 1969's *Chastity*, *Faithful* also happens to be Cher's least favorite.

When we look at her, we smile. Maybe that's all the explanation anyone needs to know.

Luke Magliaro is the co-owner of Moonstruck, a fine-dining restaurant in historic Ocean Grove, New Jersey. He is a longtime Cher fan, so when it came time to choose a name for his eating establishment, he didn't have to think twice about calling it *Moonstruck*. "I enjoyed every minute of the movie and I thought about what a great word 'Moonstruck' is," Magliaro explained "and what a great feeling being moonstruck is. Then there's all the references the movie had to love and romance and Italians and Americans as well as New York, food, and of course, Cher. The word 'moonstruck,' like the word 'Cher,' conjures up nothing but good thoughts."

When respondents were asked to cite any other big stars they regard as highly as Cher, this group claimed there was no one else that could possibly rate any higher. Without a doubt, Cher is obviously in a league of her own!

Finally, fans were asked what they would say to the pop diva if they were ever fortunate enough to meet her face-to-face. The leading response would be to thank Cher for enriching their lives. "It has been a lifelong dream of mine to meet Cher, says Terry Wayne from Detroit, Michigan. "If I did I would like to thank her for making some of the best music in the world. Cher is a true treasure. I can't imagine what my life would be like without Cher."

Dianne Jamie from Niagara Falls, Canada, added: "Cher has made me a better person. I would like to thank her for giving me so much through her music. I would like her to know she is so loved by us and we really do relate to her. I know I will always love her and look up to her as a role model." Basically the majority of respondents felt that it was their "coming of age" at the height of Cher's early popularity that many of them found comfort in her confidence and difference.

Interestingly enough, respondents also stated that they would like to talk to Cher and tell her how they feel about her and why they admire and care about her so much. "A big superstar like Cher could never imagine what a friend she has been to me over the years," says Lisa Womack. "She has really transformed my life for the better. I would do anything for her. I could never repay her for all the enjoyment and comfort her music and films have given me over these past thirty years. I only hope that Cher continues making music and pleasing her fans."

"Some people just don't 'get' the Cher thing," summed up Marie Cassatti. "What we love the most is her determination and strong sense of who she is. Cher motivates us and helps us to survive and overcome obstacles. She is a great driving force for many of us. Cher doesn't know how much she has truly given her fans since the sixties. Cher never apologizes for being Cher. She just is just Cher. When we look at her, we smile. Maybe that's all the explanation anyone needs to know."

Cher's Charity: The Children's Craniofacial Association (CCA)

Cher wholeheartedly supports the Children's Craniofacial Association—a nonprofit organization headquartered in Dallas, Texas, dedicated to improving the quality of life for people with craniofacial differences and their families. With her time, talent, and money, Cher has been CCA's most generous contributor. The organization never pursued her to be a national spokesperson, and Cher didn't seek out that role either. It was the 1985 movie *Mask*, in which Cher portrayed a mother whose son suffered from a craniofacial condition, that set the wheels in motion. *Mask* gave Cher the opportunity to see firsthand how the disease affects children and their families and springboarded her to honorary chairmanship of the CCA, a position of which she is very proud.

Cher became actively involved with CCA in 1990 when she joined medical professionals, adults, and children in Washington, D.C., for Craniofacial Awareness Week. With sincerity, warmth, and genuine empathy, Cher spent hours visiting with parents and listening to their special concerns and she also spent every available moment with the affected children, whom she calls her "kidlets."

In Washington, Cher came up with the concept of a retreat for children and their families. Cher's Annual Family Retreat Weekend, now in its twelfth year, gives families the opportunity to interact, share ideas, discuss problems and solutions, and make friends with others in a relaxed and fun atmosphere.

Over the years, Cher has developed personal relationships with many children. During her last two concert tours, she invited kids with craniofacial conditions backstage to visit. She has seen many grow from children to adults and has followed their surgeries and medical

Cher with her "kidlets" is proud to be the honorary spokesperson for CCA.

treatments. Cher frequently calls children before and after their surgeries to offer encouragement and comfort. "Cher has played a personal role in the lives of children all over the world," explains CCA's Executive Director, Charlene Smith. "She personally knows hundreds of kids and their families. She is quick to offer support to anxious parents and uplifts the spirits of the children who face many challenges throughout their lifetimes. Cher's support and encouragement has changed the lives of children who were ready to give up."

CCA's mission is to empower and give hope to facially disfigured children and their families. Cher is the perfect spokesperson and a living example of the mission statement. Celebrating CCA's national spokesperson while raising funds for Cher's favorite charity, fans have also developed ways to donate to their diva's number-one cause. For example, the first Cher Convention was held at Chicago in 2000. More than two thousand people attended the two-day Cher-fest that raised $21,000 for CCA. Organized by three fans who found each other through Cher's website, proceeds from the sale of T-shirts, photographs, and other keepsakes were donated to the Association. "Our CCA families who attended (the convention) were full of praise," noted Smith. "They raved about how everyone really went the extra mile to make the [Cher] auction successful. I have heard amazing stories about how Cher's fans honored them and how enthusiastically the fans participated in the events to support CCA."

To make a donation to the Children's Craniofacial Association, please send a check or money order to:

Children's Craniofacial Association
P.O. Box 280297
Dallas, Texas 75228
(800) 535-3643
www.ccakids.com

Cher Convention 2000

Chicago, Illinois
July 14th & 15th

CHAPTER NINETEEN

The 2000 Cher Convention Premiere

The first annual Cher Convention was held on July 14 and 15 in Chicago, Illinois, at the historic Congress Hotel. It turned out to be one of the most unparalleled experiences any Cher fan can hope to have (next to, of course, meeting her in person). A year in the making, and dubbed the "Cher-ago weekend," convention organizers and longtime fans Judy Didelot, Jody Cantwell, and Kim Werdman planned the two-day celebration of all things Cher to include live entertainment from three female impersonators (one for each decade—seventies, eighties, and nineties), dining and all-night dancing to Cher's music, Cher trivia contests, Cher seminars on music and fashion, Cher karaoke, and more. There was also a special auction of rare Cher items, and in one of the two ballrooms, several vendors set up tables to sell hundreds of Cher collectibles, including signed and unsigned photographs, albums, videos, dolls, CDs, and various rarities. All proceeds from the convention were donated to the Children's Craniofacial Association. Approximately $21,000 was raised for the organization. The only thing missing was the real Cher (though it was rumored she was in Chicago at the time).

Thanks to the Internet, Cher fans over the past few years have become connected like never before. The convention brought in fans from all over the country to celebrate the entertainer who has affected their lives on such a deeply personal level. As this book went to press, the final details for the Cher Convention 2002, to be held in Las Vegas, Nevada, on July 12 and 13 were being worked out. The organizers expect over three thousand fans of all ages and from all over the world, including the United Kingdom, Switzerland, Germany, and Russia to come and honor Cher. There were even rumors that the grand dame herself would make an appearance.

Cher Convention 2000

Friday Evening
Welcoming with cash bar
Dinner
Cher Impersonator Show
Dance

Saturday
Autograph Book
Games
Karaoke
Museum
Performances
Petitions
Seminars
Souvineers
Video and Audio Montage

Saturday Evening
Pre-dinner gathering with cash bar
Dinner
Auction
Awards and Closing Ceremonies
Dance

Old friendships and new are brought together through a common thread known as Cher.

Professional Cher impersonators
at the Chicago convention.

30 Years Later and Still...

Cher Convention 2002

July 12th, and 13th 2002
Riviera Hotel, Las Vegas
www.CherConvention.com

The Beat Goes On

Ebay auction starts September, 21st 2001

Cher Convention Registration is taking place now. Details are on our website, or send SASE to Cher Convention 2002 - 5410 S. Custer Rd. Monroe, MI 48161 An online auction of Cher items to benefit the Children's Craniofacial Association will begin September, 21st 2001. Search Ebay by seller name: CherConvention. For help with online auctions, please email questions to heathjames@aol.com.

got u babe?

A selection of Sonny & Cher items for sale.

Finding Cher on the Internet

There are literally hundreds of websites and dozens of newsgroups dedicated to Cher. There is only one official site: www.cher.com. Following is a list of the best Cher sites and related sources on the Internet as polled by over one hundred fans from around the world. Each site has key and unique content on Cher's music, life, and career. Some are like shrines, while others are exhaustive resources of Cher information.

These are in no particular order, but if you want to know what the top thirty Cher sites are on the Internet, as selected by fans, then log on to http://www.topsitelists.com/bestsites/justplaincher/topsites.html

Everything Cher
www.everythingcher.com

Just Plain Cher
www.justplaincher.com

The Power of Cher
www.angelfire.com/nc2/ThePowerofCher/
    index.html

Cher Planet
members.tripod.lycod.nl/ulixes2

Cher World.com
www.cherworld.com

Cher Castle
www.chez.com/martinezrobert/indexx.html

The Magic of Cher
geocities.com/allornothingnow2000

Cher Convention
www.cherconvention.com

Cher Glamour
www.cherglamour.com

Cher Scholar
www.cherscholar.com

Cher Extravaganza
www.cherextravaganza.com

Simply Cher
www.angelfire.com/tn/KarensPage/
    index.html

Cher Style
www.geocities.com/gabz50

Cher Palace
www.cherpalace.cjb.net

Related Cher Sites

TV Party
www.tvparty.com

TV Classics
www.tvclassics.com

The Internet's Number-One Rated Cher Newsgroup
CherNews@yahoogroups.com

Cher on Television
www.tv-now.com/stars/stars.html

or

www.RockOnTV.com

Collecting Cher (and Sonny & Cher)
www.ebay.com

Starwares
www.starwares.com

The Best of On-line Biographies, News Updates, and Miscellaneous Info on Cher

MTV On-line
www.mtv.com

All Music
www.allmusic.com

Rock on the Net
www.www.rockonthenet.com

Rolling Stone Magazine
www.rollingstone.com

VH1
www.vh1.com

Cher Convention 2000
P. O. Box 179
Dundee, MI 48131 USA

Photo by Diana

APPENDIX ONE

DISCOGRAPHY

This brief discography is not intended to be comprehensive, but merely to acknowledge Cher's (and Sonny & Cher's) standard studio and singles officially released in the United States and Canada from 1965 to the present. Many items are listed in order of release on their original recording label. Please note that many of the original recordings of full albums were also made into cassette, eight track, and CD formats. Promotional releases, foreign recordings, remixes, and miscellaneous projects have been omitted. Some "greatest hits" packages are also not listed listed. Incredibly, if we included all the United Kingdom and other European offerings on this list alone, it would contain more than a few hundred entries.

Solo Cher Album Discography
(Selective)

1965
All I Really Want to Do
Producer: Sonny Bono

1966
The Sonny Side of Cher
Producer: Sonny Bono

1967
Cher (Imperial)
Producer: Sonny Bono

1968
With Love (Imperial)
Producer: Sonny Bono

Backstage (Imperial)
Producers: Sonny Bono, Harold R. Battiste, Jr., and Denis Pregnolato

Cher's Golden Greats (Imperial)
Producer: Sonny Bono

1969
Jackson Highway (Atco)
Producers: Jerry Wexler, Tom Dowd, Arif Mardin

1971
Cher (Kapp)
Producer: Snuff Garrett

1972
Foxy Lady (Kapp)
Producers: Snuff Garrett, Sonny Bono

Cher/Superpak, Volume 1 (United Artists)
Producer: Sonny Bono

Cher/Superpak, Volume 2 (United Artists)
Producer: Sonny Bono

1973
Bittersweet White Light (MCA)
Producer: Sonny Bono

Half Breed (MCA)
Producer: Snuff Garrett

1974
Dark Lady (MCA)
Producer: Snuff Garrett

Cher's Greatest Hits (MCA)
Producer: Snuff Garrett

1975
Stars (MCA)
Producer: Jimmy Webb

The Very Best of Cher (United Artists)
Producer: Sonny Bono

Golden Hits of Cher (United Artists)

1976
I'd Rather Believe in You (Warner Brothers Records)
Producers: Steve Barri, Michael Omartian

1977
Cherished (Warner Brothers Records)
Producer: Snuff Garrett

1978
This Is Cher (Pickwick)

1979
Take Me Home (Casablanca Records)
Producer: Bob Esty

1980
Prisoner (Casablanca Records)
Producer: Bob Esty

1982
I Paralyze (Columbia))
Producer: David Wolfert

1987
Cher (Geffen Records)
Producers: Michael Bolton, Desmond Child, Jon Bon Jovi, Richie Sambora, Peter Asher

1989
Heart of Stone (Geffen Records—issued with two different covers)
Producers: Peter Asher, Michael Bolton, Desmond Child, Jon Lind, Diane Warren, Guy Roche

1991
Love Hurts (Geffen Records)
Producers: Peter Asher, Richie Zito, Bob Rock, Guy Roche, Diane Warren, Steve Lukather

1992
Half Breed (MCA Records)
Producer: Snuff Garrett, Sonny Bono

"Bang Bang" and Other Hits (EMI/Capitol Records)
Producer: Sonny Bono

1996

It's a Man's World (Reprise Records)
Producers: Sam Ward, Christopher Neil,
    Greg Penny, Stephen Lipson, Trevor Horn

Cher: The Casablanca Years
Producer: Bob Esty, Ron Dante

1998

Believe (Warner Brothers Records)
Producers: Rob Dickens, Mark Taylor, Brian
    Rawling, Junior Vasquez, Todd Terry

1999

If I Could Turn Back Time/Cher's Greatest Hits
    (Geffen Records)

Bittersweet: The Love Songs Collection (MCA
    Records)
Producers: Sonny Bono, Snuff Garrett

Bang Bang: The Early Years (Imperial Records)
Producer: Sonny Bono

Take Me Home (Universal Music Records)
Producers: Bob Esty, Ron Dante, Sonny Bono

2000

The Best of Cher: The Millennium Collection
    (MCA Records)
Producers: Snuff Garrett, Bob Esty

not.com.mercial (Artist Direct Records)
(This album is available on the Internet only,
    through Cher's official website and
    ArtistDirect.com)
Producers: Cher, Bruce Roberts

The Way of Love (MCA Records)
Producers: Snuff Garrett, Sonny Bono,
    Denis Pregnoloto, Bob Esty

2001

Essential Collection (Hip-O-Records)

2002

Living Proof (Warner Brothers Records)
Producers: Rob Dickens, Mark Taylor,
    Brian Rawling, Nick Bracegirdel, J. Aberg,
    A. Hasson, Bruce Roberts

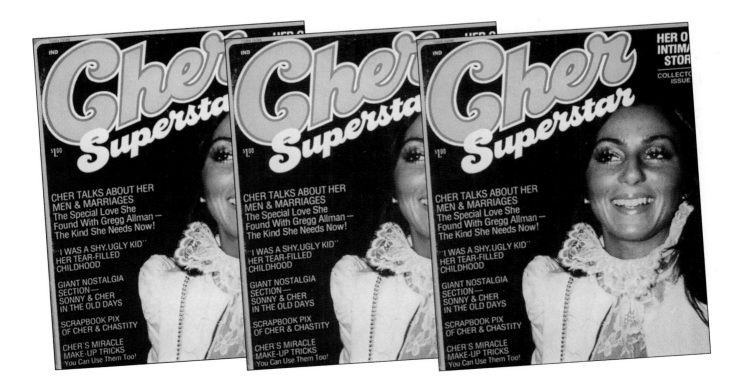

CHER SINGLES RELEASED IN THE UNITED STATES AND CANADA

1965

"Ringo I Love You" (Sceptor)
(Cher as Bonnie Jo Mason)

"Dream Baby" (Imperial Records)
(Cher as Cherilyn)

"All I Really Want to Do" (Imperial Records)
"Where Do You Go" (Imperial Records)

1966

"Bang Bang (My Baby Shot Me Down) (Imperial Records)
"Alfie" (Imperial Records)
"I Feel Something in the Air" (Liberty)
"Sunny" (Liberty)
"Behind the Door" (Imperial Records)
"Mama (When My Dollies Have Babies)" (Imperial Records)

1967

"Hey Joe" (Imperial Records)
"You'd Better Sit Down, Kids" (Imperial Records)

1968

"The Click Song" (Imperial Records)
"Take Me for a Little While" (Imperial Records)
"You'd Better Sit Down, Kids" (Liberty Records)
"Yours Until Tomorrow" (Atco Records)

1969

"I Walk on Gilded Splinters" (Atlantic Records)
"Chastity's Song" (Atco Records)
"For What It's Worth" (Atco Records)
"You've Made Me So Very Happy" (Atlantic Records)

1970

"Superstar" (Atco Records)

1971

"Lay Baby Lay" (Atco Records)
"Gypsies, Tramps, and Thieves" (Kapp)
"Don't Put It on Me" (MCA Records)
"Will You Love Me Tomorrow" (United Artists)

1972

"The Way of Love" (Kapp)
"Living in a House Divided" (Kapp)
"Don't Hide Your Love" (Kapp)

1973

"How Long Has This Been Going On?" (MCA Records)
"Am I Blue?" (MCA Records)
"Half Breed" (MCA Records)

1974

"Dark Lady" (MCA Records)
"Train of Thought" (MCA Records)

"I Saw a Man and He Danced with His Wife"
  (MCA Records)
"Carousel Man" (MCA Records)

1975
"These Days" (Warner Bros.)
"Rescue Me" (MCA Records)
"A Love Like Yours" (Duet with Nilsson) (Phil
  Spector International)

1976
"Long Distance Love Affair" (Warner Bros.)
"A Woman's Story" (Warner/Spector Records)
"Borrowed Time" (Warner Bros.)

1977
"Warpaint and Soft Feathers" (Warner Bros.)
"Pirate" (Warner Bros.)

1979
Take Me Home" (Casablanca Records)
"Wasn't It Good" (Casablanca Records)
"It's Too Late to Love Me Now" (Casablanca
  Records)
"Hell on Wheels" (Casablanca Records)
"Prisoner" (Casablanca Records)

1980
"Holdin' Out for Love" (Casablanca Records)

1982
"Rudy" (Columbia Records)
"Gypsies, Tramps, and Thieves" (Old Gold
  Records)
"I Paralyze" (CBS Records)

1984
"Bang Bang" (EMI Records)

1987
"I Found Someone" (Geffen Records)
"We All Sleep Alone" (Geffen Records)

1988
"Skin Deep" (Geffen Records)
"Main Man" (Geffen Records)

1989
"If I Could Turn Back Time" (Geffen Records)
"Gypsies, Tramps, and Theives" (Old Gold
  Records)

1990
"Just Like Jesse James" (Geffen Records)
"Heart of Stone" (Geffen Records)
"You Wouldn't Know Love" (Geffen Records)
"Baby I'm Yours" (Geffen Records)

1991
"The Shoop Shoop Song (It's in His Kiss)"
  (Geffen Records)
"Love and Understanding" (Geffen Records)
"Save Up All Your Tears" (Geffen Records)

1992
Oh, No, Not My Baby" (Geffen Records)

1993
"Many Rivers to Cross (Geffen Records)
"Whenever You're Near" (Geffen Records)

1995
"Love Can Build a Bridge" (with Chrissie Hynde
  and Neneh Cherry) (London Records)
"Walking in Memphis" (Reprise Records)

1996
"One by One" (Reprise Records)
"Paradise Is Here" (Reprise Records)

1998
"Believe" (Warner Bros.)

1999
"Strong Enough" (Warner Bros.)
"All or Nothing" (Warner Bros.)
"Dov'è l'Amore" (Warner Bros.)

2002
"(This Is) a Song for the Lonely" (Warner Bros.)
"The Music's No Good Without You" (Warner
  Bros.)

SONNY & CHER: THE SINGLES

1965

Sonny & Cher (as Caesar & Cleo)

"Do You Wanna Dance" (Reprise Records)

"Love Is Strange" (Reprise Records)

"Let the Good Times Roll" (Reprise Records)

Sonny & Cher

"Baby Don't Go" (Reprise Records Records)

"The Letter" (Vault Records)

"Just You" (Atco Records)

"I Got You Babe" (Atco Records)

"What Now My Love" (Atco Records)

"But You're Mine" (Atco Records)

1966

"What Now My Love" (Atco Records)

"Have I Stayed Too Long?" (Atco Records)

"Little Man" (Atco Records)

"Living for You" (Atco Records)

1967

"The Beat Goes On" (Atco Records)

"Beautiful Story" (Atco Records)

"Plastic Man" (Atco Records)

"Podunk" (Atco Records)

"It's the Little Things" (Atco Records)

"Don't Talk to Strangers" (Atco Records)

1968

"Good Combination" (Atco Records)

"You Gotta Have a Thing of Your Own Babe" (Atco Records)

1970

"Get It Together" (Atlantic Records)

1971

"Real People" (MCA Records)

"All I Ever Need Is You" (Kapp Records)

"Somebody" (Kapp Records)

1972

"A Cowboy's Work Is Never Done" (Kapp Records)

"When You Say Love" (Kapp Records)

"Mama Was a Rock and Roll Singer, Papa Used to Write All Her Songs" (Part One) (MCA)

"The Greatest Show on Earth" (MCA)

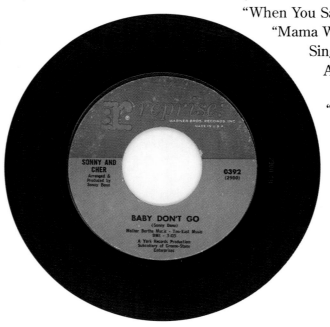

SONNY & CHER: THE ALBUMS

(Selective)

1965

Look at Us (Atco Records)
Producer: Sonny Bono

1966

The Wondrous World of Sonny & Cher (Atco)
Producer: Sonny Bono

1967

In Case You're in Love (Atco Records)
Producer: Sonny Bono

Good Times Original Film Soundtrack (Atco Records)
Producer: Sonny Bono

The Best of Sonny & Cher (Atco Records)
Producer: Sonny Bono

1971

Sonny & Cher Live (MCA Records)
Producer: Denis Pregnolato

1972

All I Ever Need Is You (MCA Records)
Producer: Snuff Garrett

1973

Mama Was a Rock and Roll Singer, Papa Used to Write All Her Songs (MCA Records)
Producers: Denis Pregnolato, Michael Rubini, Sonny Bono

Sonny & Cher Live in Las Vegas (Volume 2) (MCA Records)
Producer: Denis Pregnolato

The Two of Us (Atco Records)
Producer: Sonny Bono

1975

The Beat Goes On (Atco Records)
Producers: Sonny Bono, Jerry Wexler, Tom Dowd and Arif Mardin

Greatest Hits (MCA Records)
Producers: Denis Pregnolato, Snuff Garrett, Michael Rubini, and Sonny Bono

1990

All I Ever Need Is You (MCA Records)
Producers: Snuff Garrett, Sonny Bono, and Denis Pregnolato

1991

The Beat Goes On: The Best of Sonny & Cher (Atco Records)
Producer: Sonny Bono

1993

I Got You Babe (Rhino Records)
Producer: Sonny Bono

1995

All I Ever Need: The Kapp/MCA Anthology (MCA Records)
Producers: Snuff Garrett, Sonny Bono, Denis Pregnolato, and Michael Rubini

1997

"I Got You Babe" and Other Hits (Atlantic Records)
Producer: Sonny Bono

1998

Sonny & Cher Greatest Hits (Uni/MCA Records)
Producers: Sonny Bono, Snuff Garrett, Denis
   Pregnolato

Look at Us (Sundazed Records) (includes bonus
   tracks)
Producer: Sonny Bono

The Wonderous World of Sonny & Cher (Sundazed
   Records) (includes bonus tracks)
Producer: Sonny Bono

In Case You're in Love (Sundazed Records)
   (includes bonus tracks)
Producer: Sonny Bono

1999

Good Times (Atlantic Recording Group)
producer: Sonny Bono

CHER GUEST VOCALS ON OTHER ARTISTS' ALBUMS AND MOVIE SOUNDTRACKS

Cher and Greg Allman as Allman & Woman

1977
Two the Hard Way (Warner Bros. Records)
Producers: Johnny Sandlin, Greg Allman and
   John Haeny

1980
Cher and Les Dudek & Band as Black Rose
Black Rose (Casablanca Records)
Producer: James Newton-Howard

- - - - - - - -

Cher as Guest Vocalist on Other Artists' Albums

1978
Gene Simmons (Casablanca Records)
Song: "Living in Sin"

1980
Foxes (Original soundtrack by various artists)
   (Casablanca Records)
Song: "Bad Love"

1981
Dead Ringer (Epic Records)
Song: "Dead Ringer for Love," with Meatloaf

1990
Mermaids (Original soundtrack by various
   artists)
"The Shoop Shoop Song"
"Baby I'm Yours"

1993
Beavis and Butt-head (Geffen Records)
Song: "I Got You Babe," with Beavis and
   Butt-head

1994
The Glory of Gershwin (various artists) (Mercury
   Records)
Song: "It Ain't Necessarily So," with Larry Adler

1996
For Our Children, Too (various artists) (Kid
   Rhino Records)
Song: "A Dream Is a Wish Your Heart Makes"

1999
Sing America (various artists) (Arista Records)
Song: "Star-Spangled Banner"

VH1 Divas Live '99 (various artists) (Arista
   Records)
Songs: "Proud Mary," with Tina Turner and
   Elton John
"If I Could Turn Back Time"

A Rosie Christmas (Rosie O'Donnell) (Columbia
   Records)
Song: "Christmas (Baby Please Come Home)"

$5.95 (U.S.), $6.95 (CAN.), £4.95 (U.K.), Y2,500 (JAPAN)

NEWSPAPER

Billboard.

THE INTERNATIONAL NEWSWEEKLY OF MUSIC, VIDEO, AND HOME ENTERTAINMENT

JANUARY 22, 2000

ACKNOWLEDGMENTS

This book would not have been possible without the invaluable assistance of entertainment journalists Anne Raso and Carrie Fascia. Thanks to Judy Black, Richard Fenkel, and Jamie Cassata for their various research duties. For their considerable efforts, special thanks and hugs go to Wayne Smith, Heidi Thompson, Mark Bego, J. Randi Taraborrelli, Charles Casillo, Jody Cantwell, Kim Werdman, Charlene Smith, Chuck Swift, Marcia Tysseling, Bill Morgan, Greg Loesher, Cathy Bernardi, Tim Neely, Renee Daigle, and Florence Hornberger.

For those who openly shared their Cher and Sonny & Cher memories, collections, and personal photographs, I salute you: Rose DelGardo, Pam Roberts, Sue Retallick, Josie Caruso Sethi, John Hostetler, Ward Lamb, Erle D. Haskin, Luis Aguilar, R. De Silva, Bert Marino, Gabrielle Dragan, and Gerri Priest.

For all the new friends I've met through the writing of *The Cher Scrapbook*, thank you all for your generosity, encouragement and unfailing spirits. A gracious nod goes to ever dedicated and tireless Cher Convention staff. You guys rock! Can't wait for the next one!

Also thanks to my ever-clever agent, Jim Fitzgerald, for once again making it all possible. I would also like to gratefully acknowledge my extremely patient publisher, Bruce Bender, and equally understanding editor, Margaret Wolf. And I can't forget my longtime friend Lisa Wagner for her endless moral and emotional support and who, by the way, fits perfectly into all the Cher clothes I buy from Starwares! Finally, I wish to acknowledge Cher herself, who over the years has provided the world with her incomparable talent and who never disappoints her fans and never ceases to amaze and delight us all!

Sources

Information for this book has been obtained from various sources including: record, television, and film companies: Atco Records, Atlantic Records, Imperial Records, MCA Records, Geffen Records, Universal Records, Reprise Records, Casablanca Records, Warner Brothers Records, Rhino Records, Sundazed Records, HBO, MGM Films, Miramax Films, Cinecom Films, Metro-Goldwyn-Mayer Films, Columbia Pictures, Orion Films, MGM, CBS Television, ABC Television, Hullabaloo, New Line Cinema, Tri-Star Pictures, ABC Motion Pictures, Warner Brothers Films, and Universal Studios.

The author also used her own personal interviews, published stories, and press-conference material with Sonny Bono, Cher, and industry insiders indirectly involved with Cher. This book was not authorized or sponsored by Cher.

Other sources include:

People, US, Time, TV Guide, Rolling Stone, Life, Playboy, Sterling magazines, *Ray Gun,* VH1, *Los Angeles Times, The New York Times, New York Daily News, New York Magazine, The Times* (London), *Newsweek, Song Hits, Hit Parader, American Songwriter, Goldmine, Cher Superstar Magazine,*

Cher Exposed Magazine, *Ladies' Home Journal*, *Vanity Fair*, *Woman's World*, *Houston Chronicle*, *The Herald Sun*, The BBC Network, *Orlando Sentinel*, *Grit* newspaper, The Learning Channel, *Dateline*, Children's Craniofacial Association, *HX*, *The Toronto Sun*, Sanctuary catalog, *Antique Trader*, and Reuters/*Variety* and *The Gay Advocate*.

Books:

Cher, If You Believe by Mark Bego (Cooper Square Press, 2001)

The First Time by Cher (Simon & Schuster, 1998)

Cher! by Mark Bego (Pocket Books, 1986)

Cher by J. Randy Taraborrelli (St. Martin's Press, 1986)

Totally Uninhibited: The Life and Wild Times of Cher by Lawrence J. Quirk (Morrow, 1991)

Cher: the Visual Documentary by Nigel Goodall (Omnibus Press, 1992)

Cher: In Her Own Words by Chris Charlesworth (Omnibus Press, 1992)

Dressing for Glamour by Bob Mackie (A&W Publishers, 1979)

Unmistakingly Mackie: The Fashion and Fantasy of Bob Mackie, by Frank DeCaro (Universe Publishers, 1999)

The Operator: David Geffen Builds, Buys, and Sells the New Hollywood by Tom King (Random House, 2000)

Kiss and Make Up by Gene Simmons (Crown Publishers, 2001)

Leonard Maltin's Movie Guide (Signet, 2001)

Websites:

E! Online, Rollingstone.com, CDnow.com, Cher.com, imbd.com, YahooMusic.com, CherConvention.com, Cherworld.com, Justplaincher.com, Cher Extravaganza, eBay.com, Amazon.com, Mattel.com, Rhinohandmade.com, and TVparty.com

Photo Credits

Unless noted, many photos and other reproductions in this book are courtesy of Atco Records, Atlantic Records, Imperial Records, MCA Records, Geffen Records, Universal Records, Reprise Records, Casablanca Records, Warner Brothers Records, Rhino Records, Sundazed Records, HBO, MGM Films, Miramax Films, Cinecom Films, Metro-Goldwyn-Mayer Films, Columbia Pictures, Orion Films, MGM, CBS Television, ABC Television, Hullabaloo, New Line Cinema, Tri-Star Pictures, ABC Motion Pictures, Warner Brothers Films, and Universal Studios.

Other credits include: Time-Life Magazines, Prime Media Magazines, *Saturday Evening Post, In the Know, Screen Stars, PhotoPlay, TV Radio Mirror, Movie World, Time, US, People, After Dark, Cosmopolitan, Details, New Woman, Ms., Ladies' Home Journal, Vanity Fair, Newsweek, TV Host, New York Magazine, Premiere, Hollywood Then and Now, Parade, New Woman, Sanctuary, CD Music & Audio Reviews, Entertainment Weekly, TV Guide, Celebrity Style, Billboard, TV Talk*. All other images and print memorabilia provided by the Author's private collection; Celebrity Photos: Gilbert Flores, Janet Gough, Scott Downie, Roger Karnbad, Kevin Winter, John Paschal, Peter Kramer; "Bang Bang" courtesy of Cotillion Music; "Strong Enough" courtesy of Warner Bros.; "Half Breed" courtesy of KAPP/MCA Records; PhotoFest, Al Pereira, Fred Zott, David Sigler, Steven Miller, Marc Culver, Keith Roberts, John Hosteler, Kim Werdman, Brad Wright, Dawn Quick, Sue Retallick, Josie Sethi, Ericka De Ciutus, Barbara Lorenz, and Rick Gillar.

In addition, the author graciously acknowledges photographs and other reproductions with kind "permission to reprint granted by": *American Songwriter* magazine, *Goldmine*, Billboard Publications, Mark Bego, J. Randy Taraborrelli, Wayne Smith, Heidi Thompson, Ward Lamb, Paul Gallo, Pam Roberts, Kim Werdman (Cher Convention), Charlene Smith (Children's Craniofacial Association), Bill Morgan (TV toys), and Chuck Swift.

Every effort has been made to identify the copyright owners of the pictures used in this publication. The author and publisher apologize for any omissions and will make proper corrections in future editions.

ABOUT THE AUTHOR

Mary Anne Cassata is a celebrated entertainment writer much intrigued by pop culture. She has collected and traded Sonny & Cher memorabilia for over thirty years. Mary Anne edits two popular teen magazines, *Teen Dream* and *Faces in Rock*, and she writes regularly for a variety of national entertainment publications. She has written biographies of Cher, the Monkees, Michael J. Fox, Jonathan Taylor Thomas, Alicia Silverstone, 'Nsync, and other celebrities. She is also the author of *The Elton John Scrapbook* (2002). This is her second book on Cher.